Above Brooklyn Bridge Park (p118)

BEST BIRDING
These NYC bird-watching spots can't be beat:
Central Park (p44)
Pelham Bay Park, Bronx
Prospect Park (p130)
MoMa Sculpture Garden (p54)

GREEN SPACES
GALORE

New York City is known for being a city of steel, concrete, roads and subways. But the 1700 well-appointed parks sprinkled throughout all five boroughs are a verdant counterpoint. In addition to the epic expanse of Central Park, the city's most famous park, hundreds more are available for a relaxing walk, jog, picnic or gathering.

→ SECRET GARDENS

One of the best ways to experience New York City's greenery is through the local community gardens hidden in secret places throughout the city.

Left Red northern cardinal, Central Park **Right** Bird bath, Conservatory Garden, Central Park **Below** Hudson River Park

CONCRETE CANOPIES

Gorgeous constructed green spaces like Little Island (p69) and the High Line (p70) underscore New York's incredible efforts to promote sustainable architecture.

Best Green-Space Experiences

▶ Take in Central Park, the city's largest, ranging from 59th to 110th Sts. (p44)

▶ Gaze at the iconic Manhattan skyline from Brooklyn Bridge Park. (p118)

▶ Walk through the famed arch at Washington Square Park. (p84)

▶ Catch a spontaneous jam session in Tompkins Square Park. (p136)

↑ RIVER VIEWS

Riverside green spaces such as Hudson River Park (p68) in the West Village offer perfect water views from Manhattan's shores.

PICK YOUR
SKYLINE

New York City boasts dozens of spectacular aerial views to choose from. Whether you're interested in a view of the mighty Brooklyn Bridge from Lower Manhattan, or the sweeping views of the city from the top the Empire State Building and the One World Observatory (p97) at One World Trade Center, prepare to be inspired.

VITEZSLAV VALKA/SHUTTERSTOCK ©

Left One World Observatory
Right View from Empire State
Building **Below** View from
Whitney Museum of Art

→ NEW YORK IN PANORAMA

With one of the most iconic aerial views in the city, the Empire State Building (p58) offers panoramic views of Central Park, Midtown and Downtown.

DOWNTOWN PIERS

Pier 17 (p91) in the Financial District provides one of the finest views of the Brooklyn Bridge from Manhattan.

Views from Every Angle

▶ Get your West Side water views at peaceful Hudson River Park. (p68)

▶ Enjoy stunning views of the New York City skyline from Brooklyn Bridge Park. (p118)

▶ Marvel at top-notch Statue of Liberty views from Tribeca's Pier A. (p91)

RIGHT: ARTYOORAN/SHUTTERSTOCK ©,
LEFT: F11PHOTO/SHUTTERSTOCK ©

↑ WEST & DOWN

Downtown areas of the West Side allow for beautiful views, most notably from the Standard Hotel and the Whitney Museum of American Art (p70).

THE NYC DINING
EXPERIENCE

▬▬▬ Savor phenomenal cuisine from almost every country on the planet and across all genres, regions and flavor profiles. Whether you're looking for a seven-course meal, a casual hot dog to eat while you walk, the perfect gelato or the best bagel of your life – New York City dining offers what you seek.

DRAGON FRUIT 627
紅肉火龍果
$4.99/LB

→ QUINTESSENTIAL QUEENS

Flushing, Queens, is home to one of the world's best Chinatowns (p185), complete with homemade delights from almost every region of China.

Left Katz's Delicatessen (p141) **Right** Market stall, Chinatown, Flushing, Queens **Below** Manhattan cocktail

BAGEL BONANZA

New York as a whole is known for its epic bagels, but Zabar's (p43) and Black Seed Bagels (p147) are absolute must-tries.

↑ MARTINIS & MANHATTANS

Manhattan has a drink named after it for a reason. This borough's swanky cocktails are the ultimate 'drinker's drinks.' Take a swig!

Browse the City's Best

▶ Visit Queens, the most diverse urban neighborhood in the world, for global food options galore. (p184)

▶ Some of the top bagel joints in town are in the Lower East Side and East Village. (p140)

▶ Dine in style at a cozy Greenwich Village restaurant or riverside wine bar. (p85)

▶ Get your vino and appetizers on at a swanky downtown wine or tapas bar in Tribeca. (p96)

PUBLIC INDOOR
PALACES

In New York City, some of the most stunning architectural displays and most palatial interiors aren't for the select few – they're hiding in plain sight and accessible to all visitors of the city. From the iconic ceiling of Grand Central Terminal to the marbled halls of the New York Public Library, give your eyes a show in some of New York City's greatest gilded halls.

Left New York Public Library
Right Grand Central Terminal
Below Trinity Church

→ **GRAND CENTRAL TERMINAL**
In addition to being a transit hub teeming with local commuters, Grand Central Terminal is a true marvel of modern architecture.

GREAT LIBRARIES
The New York Public Library and the Morgan Library and Museum (p59) will be a satisfying experience for both book-lovers and museum-lovers.

↑ **THE MAGIC OF CHURCHES**
New York's churches are absolutely divine – particularly Old St Patrick's Cathedral (p148), Trinity Church (p93) and Plymouth Church (p125).

Dreamy Interiors

▶ Ogle one of Frank Lloyd Wright's finest exteriors at the Guggenheim Museum. (p155)

▶ Explore the Metropolitan Museum of Art's gleaming halls for hours. (p154)

▶ Enjoy the plush velvet and brocade interiors of the Morgan Library and Museum. (p59)

▶ Murmur a prayer of thanks for the incomparable beauty of St Patrick's Cathedral. (p61)

HONORING THE FALLEN

FDNY Memorial
(Greenwich St, Financial District)

NYC Police Memorial
(Liberty St, Financial District)

Korean War Memorial
(the Battery, Financial District)

Vietnam Veterans Plaza
(Water St, Financial District)

POWERFUL
MEMORIALS

▬▬ From the arrival of the Statue of Liberty as a gift from France to the welcoming of Irish immigrants, and the respect and honor shown to the city's fallen firefighters and civilians after 9/11, New York City has many emotional moments to remember. Dozens of beautiful memorials keep this history alive and cherished.

Noble Histories

▶ Pay your respects at the National September 11 Memorial & Museum. (p92)

▶ Crane your neck to see One World Trade Center's soaring Freedom Tower. (p92)

▶ Absorb Harlem history at Schomburg Center of Black Research. (p173)

▶ Enjoy a history lesson at Grant's Tomb on the Upper West Side. (p39; pictured)

RYAN D BUDHU/GETTY IMAGES ©

↘ FASHION'S MAIN DRAGS

Madison Ave On the Upper East Side.

Fifth Ave Between 50th and 59th Sts in Midtown.

SoHo 14th St to Canal St on the East and West Sides.

Check out the Museum at FIT experience on p76.

RALPH LAUREN

Best Shopping Experiences

▶ Stop by Pippin Vintage Jewelry for an unforgettable sparkly experience. (p78)

▶ Peruse the racks at Kirna Zabete, great for label-lovers and European-leaning tastes. (p112)

▶ Check out the quirky and colorful peacock wallflower at Yumi Kim. (p164)

▶ Count on Ralph Lauren to offer classic American design. (p164; pictured)

SHOP UNTIL **YOU DROP**

■■■ If you're looking for a shopping experience like none other, New York City will fulfill your wildest dreams. It's one of the fashion capitals of the world, and every street is your own personal runway. Whether strolling through Manhattan's Uptown, Midtown or Downtown, there's truly a street for every style.

IT'S WINE
O'CLOCK!

New York City has a thriving, jam-packed pub and bar culture; its wine scene, however, is truly a sight to behold. You can find wine offerings from almost every region in the world and a flavor profile for every palate. Bars often offer tasty tapas and small plates to bring out the best in each wine. Enjoy!

Cheers to That!

▶ Try a glass of wine overlooking Hudson River Park at City Winery. (p85)

▶ Toast with a glass of bubbly at cozy wine bar Ruffian in the East Village. (p147)

▶ Grab a few bottles of vino from Uva then walk over to Central Park for a picnic and toast. (p165)

★ LATE-NIGHT WINES

Complete with a late-night menu served until 2am and a particularly impressive wine list, Uva is the ultimate Uptown staple.

← SOUTH AFRICAN WINE FLAVORS

New York City's wine culture is remarkable for its variety. A hidden favorite is Kaia Wine Bar, which specializes in South African wines and food.

Top left Wine in front of Manhattan skyline
Bottom left City Winery

BOOZY BARS & BEERS

Known for its glitz, glamour and sparkle, NYC is also home to hole-in-the-wall dive bars with a charm all their own. Nightly 'beer and a shot' specials hit the spot before a fun night out, or put some coins in an old-school juke box to set the mood. Read on for the ultimate dive-bar experience in the city that never sleeps.

LEFT: VALERY RIZZO/ALAMY STOCK PHOTO © BOTTOM: ANTONELLA SPINELLI/EYEEM/GETTY IMAGE ©

★ CLASSIC COCKTAIL BARS

Manhattan has truly excellent cocktail bars to try. Little Branch (p85) is the toast of Downtown cocktails, while 67 Orange (p178) has a fine list of signature cocktails like the 'Santa Rockey.' For vodka, Russian Vodka Room (p63) is prime.

Best Dive Bars

▶ Check out Ryan's Daughter on the Upper East Side, slinging drinks since 1979. (p163)

▶ Enjoy the laid-back vibe and twinkling Christmas lights at Biddy's Pub. (p163)

▶ Stop by Lucky, an East Village dive with excellent specials and a rocking crowd. (p137)

▶ Have a beer on the balcony at Five Mile Stone and watch the passers-by. (p163)

← WILLIAMSBURG'S CRAFT-BEER SCENE

Williamsburg, Brooklyn, has endless allure and a sophisticated craft-beer scene (p126). Try Talea for a fruit-forward list, while Grimm Artisanal Ales has experimental sours and flavors on hand.

Top left Beer, Strong Rope Brewery, Williamsburg
Bottom left Cocktails

NEW YORK CITY BEST EXPERIENCES

↓ **Central Park**

Summerstage in Central Park often hosts free concerts with a full schedule available on its website, or try to catch a play at Shakespeare in the Park.

▶ cityparksfoundation.org/summerstage

↓ **Tribeca Film Festival**

Catch an indie film at the famous Tribeca Film Festival. You may even spot a celebrity or two.

📍 Tribeca; p95

▶ tribecafilm.com

↓ **Fourth of July**

There are lots of parties at premier rooftop lounges with the best vantage points overlooking East River fireworks, so book tickets at popular venues a week or two in advance.

JUNE

June average daytime max:
80°F (27°C)
Days of rainfall: 8

JULY

Summer in NYC can be humid. Wear light clothes. Duck into stores to stay cool during excursions.

New York in
SUMMER

Rooftop lounges are popular hangout destinations during this season, particularly in hotels across downtown Manhattan and Brooklyn.

↓ Afropunk

Afropunk happens every August in Brooklyn. Weekend street fairs pop up in various neighborhoods from Midtown to Chelsea. There's also Queens Night Market in Flushing's Chinatown.

↗ Beaches

For sun and sand visit beach enclaves like Rockaway Beach in Queens, Coney Island and Manhattan Beach in Brooklyn, or day trip to the Hamptons.

NEW YORK CITY PLAN BY SEASON

AUGUST

July average daytime max:
84°F (29°C)
Days of rainfall: 8

August average daytime max:
84°F (29°C)
Days of rainfall: 7

Summer is peak season, so expect long lines and crowds at popular tourist spots and landmarks. Hotels are also more expensive.

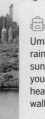

Packing notes

Umbrella for sporadic rains, sunscreen and sunglasses to protect yourself from the heat, and comfortable walking shoes.

Check out the full calendar of events

→ Labor Day Weekend

From the West Indian Day parade in Brooklyn to enjoying the last day to soak in the sun on the beach, Labor Day Weekend has no shortage of events and parties to partake in.

↙ Fashion Week

Every September Fashion Week takes place, so beware extra traffic congestion at popular locations around Manhattan, especially early to mid-September.
▶ nyfw.com

← San Gennaro Festival

At Little Italy's San Gennaro Festival vendors sell Italian sweets and snacks in addition to alcoholic beverages alongside carnival games.
● Little Italy; p149
▶ sangennaronyc.org

Visit city parks like Central Park in Manhattan or Prospect Park in Brooklyn to capture beautiful photos of fall foliage.

SEPTEMBER

September average daytime max:
76°F (24°C)
Days of rainfall: 7

OCTOBER

New York in
FALL

↙ Thanksgiving Eve

Thanksgiving will have a handful of restaurants open for families looking to dine out for the holiday. Don't miss Thanksgiving Eve parties at different hot spots in popular nightlife areas like the Meatpacking District.

↑ Halloween & Thanksgiving

Join the annual Halloween Parade in downtown Manhattan and party at pop-up events that mark the occasion.

NEW YORK CITY PLAN BY SEASON

NOVEMBER

October average daytime max:
64°F (18°C)
Days of rainfall: 6

November average daytime max:
55°F (13°C)
Days of rainfall: 7

🎒 Packing notes

Bring your best fall jackets and comfortable boots. Don't forget your camera to capture the beautiful fall foliage.

↓ Window Displays

Travel to Midtown and walk between the beautiful Christmas-themed window displays at stores such as Saks, Macy's and Bloomingdales.

↓ Christmas Markets

Christmas brings a new vibe to the city and there's lots to indulge in. Visit the Christmas markets in Bryant Park by Times Square or by Union Square or Columbus Circle.

↓ NYE Party Planning

Purchase your event tickets at least a month in advance for the best rate, especially at popular venues, and be prepared for surge pricing when traveling at night via taxi.

DECEMBER

December average daytime max:
44°F (7°C)
Days of rainfall: 8

JANUARY

New York in
WINTER

← Times Square Ball Drop

Get to Times Square early if you plan to see the ball drop on New Year's Eve. Dress warm and be prepared to stand for several hours.

January tends to be the coldest month, but it's also the slowest for tourism. It's a great time to see popular sights without the large crowds.

↙ Ice-Skating Rinks

Visit Rockefeller Center to see the famous Christmas tree, then go ice skating at its rink. Skate also at Bryant Park and Brookfield Place near the World Trade Center.

The city has its share of snowstorms and snow can persist for weeks on the sidewalks. Bring proper footwear to get around easier.

NEW YORK CITY PLAN BY SEASON

FEBRUARY

January average daytime max:
39°F (4°C)
Days of rainfall: 8

February average daytime max:
43°F (6°C)
Days of rainfall: 7

🎒 Packing notes

Wear your warmest coats and bring hats and gloves to stay warm, along with a pair of reliable snow boots.

Spring is the city's wet season, so expect rain, specifically during April and early May.

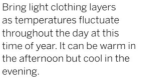

Bring light clothing layers as temperatures fluctuate throughout the day at this time of year. It can be warm in the afternoon but cool in the evening.

↖ Spring Flowers

Visit the different gardens around the city for the spring activation events. You can even see the cherry blossoms bloom at the Brooklyn Botanical Garden in early April.

MARCH

March average daytime max:
52°F (11°C)
Days of rainfall: 8

APRIL

New York in
SPRING

↓ Baseball Season

Baseball season begins! Check the schedule, buy tickets and head to Yankee Stadium in the Bronx for a game.

● The Bronx

▶ mlb.com/yankees

↘ Memorial Day

Memorial Day weekend marks the opening of New York beaches and the start of summer, with tons of parties scheduled for the three-day weekend.

May is allergy season, so you may experience symptoms, especially if staying near a park with a high pollen count. Visit a pharmacy for over-the-counter medication.

NEW YORK CITY PLAN BY SEASON

April average daytime max:
64°F (18°C)
Days of rainfall: 8

MAY

May average daytime max:
72°F (22°C)
Days of rainfall: 9

🎒 Packing notes

Pack a light versatile raincoat with an umbrella for rainy days, along with allergy medication for seasonal pollen.

MY PERFECT DAY IN
NEW YORK CITY

By Dana Givens
@ @danawritesalot

CULTURE, FUN & ART

On a sunny day I breakfast or brunch at Sarabeth's on the Upper West Side. From there, I walk through Central Park before spending time at the Metropolitan Art Museum browsing the Costume exhibit and other favorite sections. Once done, I head downtown to East Village and hang out around St Mark's Place, grabbing a bite at one of the small Japanese restaurants like Kenka. After dinner, I continue to W 4th St for a comedy show and drinks at the Fat Black Pussycat.

↙ BEST UNIQUE ART & MUSEUM EXPERIENCES
Head to Chelsea for the Museum of Sex, then West Village for the Museum of Ice Cream (p113). Try Spyscape in Midtown to feel like James Bond for a day.

Please do not touch, lick, stroke or mount the exhibits.

museumofse**x**

...AMONG THE LOTUS

Above left Museum of Sex **Above right** Museum of Ice Cream **Opposite page** High Line

DAN HERRICK/LONELY PLANET ©

DPA PICTURE ALLIANCE/ALAMY STOCK PHOTO ©

ARCHITECTURE, ART & DINING

■■■■ Lust over beautiful brownstones on a morning stroll through Brooklyn Heights while gobbling an egg galette from Poppy's. Arrive at the Brooklyn Heights Promenade (p122) to survey Manhattan's skyline, then bike the Brooklyn Bridge for epic East River views. Stop by the Meatpacking District to peep at the Whitney's (p70) permanent modern-art collection before ambling along the High Line (p70) to see swanky buildings designed by acclaimed architects. Trendy Williamsburg and beatnik Bushwick are the best answers for dinner and dancing.

By John Garry
@garryjohnfrancis

WHY I LOVE NEW YORK

New York maintains the integrity of its name by never getting old. When I think I've seen it all, the city surprises me most.

MASSIMO SALESI/SHUTTERSTOCK ©

By Harmony Difo
harmonydifo.com

FINE ART, DINING & EPIC VIEWS

■■■■ Watch the sun rise from a skyscraper overlooking Manhattan followed by brunch at a Midtown bistro. Stroll downtown to the Whitney Museum of American Art (p70) and the Chelsea galleries before perusing the High Line (p70). Enjoy sunset at Hudson River Park (p68), dinner out in the West Village and a sing-along at Marie's Crisis (p74). Check out the scene at a local punk bar, club or dive in the East Village, ending with a swanky nightcap at Bowery Hotel. Voila!

WHY I LOVE NEW YORK

New York is a gorgeous marriage of opposites: creative and wild but always professional, carefully structured but free and lawless – always the experience of a lifetime!

7 Things to Know About
NEW YORK CITY

INSIDER TIPS TO HIT THE GROUND RUNNING.

1 Carless Travel

Driving is expensive and not the time-saver you think it is, especially when traveling to places like SoHo or Midtown where parking can be expensive. Opt to travel mostly by subway to get to things faster. Instead of using Uber or Lyft, download the Curbed app to get a yellow or green taxi.

▶ For more on getting around, see p210

2 Location, Location!

Stay in a neighborhood that matches your travel style and what you want to get out of the trip. If you're intent on a nightlife-focused stay, find accommodations further downtown to be near high-profile clubs and bars. For a quieter stay, settle uptown in the Upper East Side to be near cultural institutions like museums and five-star shopping. For popular restaurants and small bars, head to the Upper West Side.

4 These Shoes Are Made for Walking

Despite the various modes of transport available, you're going to be doing a lot of walking, so bring comfortable shoes. Allow time for transit disruptions due to subway construction and maintenance.

3 Obey Sidewalk Rules

New Yorkers are fast walkers and have their own traffic rules. To avoid any trouble, keep right when walking and avoid sudden stops.

6 Subway = Best Way

Multiple subway lines connect Manhattan, Brooklyn, Queens and the Bronx. The only borough you can't take the train to is Staten Island, which is accessible by ferry. It's easy to get confused when first using the different subway lines; however, subway is the easiest way to navigate your way around NYC. Download the MyMTA app for schedules, routes and alerts on different lines. Planned service changes or delays are also accessible online (new.mta.info).

The 4/5/6 subway lines are mainly focused on stops on the east side of Manhattan, with the 4/5 trains making express stops and the 6 train making local stops. The 1/2/3 lines focus on the west side, with the 2/3 trains making express stops and the 1 train making local stops. The A/C/E and B/D/F lines focus on the west side and most southern parts of Manhattan.

5 Budget Airport Transportation

If you don't want to take an Uber or Lyft, ride the LIRR to Jamaica station, then take the AirTrain to JFK Airport. Via the MTA, take the E, J, or Z train to Sutphin Blvd-Archer Ave-JFK Airport station, follow the signs to Jamaica station, then catch the AirTrain to JFK. For LaGuardia, take the 6 train to 125th St then the M60 bus.

▶ For more on arriving in New York City, see p208

7 Best Times for Times Square

Don't plan on spending a lot of time around Times Square – it's just big-brand shopping and chain restaurants. Besides catching some shows on nearby Broadway, there's not much to do outside shopping. Wait until after 10pm to walk around to avoid battling big crowds and enjoy the ambience.

Read, Listen, Watch & Follow

📖 | **READ**

The Big Sea
(Langston Hughes;
1940) The famous
writer's memoir.

Harlem Is Nowhere
(Sharifa Rhodes-
Pitts; 2001)
Conversations with
residents about
Harlem's changing
landscape.

Up in the Old Hotel
(Joseph Mitchell;
2015) Tales of
various New Yorkers
living their daily
lives.

**Ladies and
Gentlemen: The
Bronx Is Burning**
(Jonathan Mahler;
2005) In-depth look
at the politics of
Bronx baseball.

🎧 | **LISTEN**

The Blueprint
(Jay-Z; 2001) Hip-
hop album built
on the New York
sound by one of the
genre's best artists.

**Get Rich or
Die Tryin'**
(50 Cent; 2003) An
iconic album that
changed hip-hop for
NYC's artists.

West Side Story
(Original Cast; 1957)
Famous Broadway
play of Latino living
in NYC.

Like a Virgin
(Madonna; 1983)
Legendary pop
star's album
inspired thousands
to live out their
fantasies in the city.

The Bowery Boys
(Thomas Meyers and Greg Young; 2007)
Podcast that focuses on different historic
events and figures in NYC.

▷ WATCH

Breakfast at Tiffany's (1961) Audrey Hepburn stars as a woman who falls in love with a struggling writer.

Do the Right Thing (1989) A fiery argument between residents occurs on a hot day in Brooklyn.

Annie (2014) Remake of Broadway play about an orphan adopted by a wealthy older man.

The Devil Wears Prada (2006) Inside look at what it takes to make it in NYC fashion.

Rent (2005) Remake of Broadway play about the struggles of a group of bohemian New York residents.

⊙ FOLLOW

@humansofny
Humans of New York official account.

@lovelettertonewyorkcity
NYC photography curated by travel influencer Nastasia Yakoub

@dancalders
Photographer Dan Calderwood's shots of NYC.

Alfred Pommer
(nycwalk.com) Historical walking tours across Manhattan.

@KarenBritChick
YouTuber who documents her daily routines in NYC.

↘ Sate your New York City dreaming with a virtual vacation at lonelyplanet.com/new-york-city

UPPER WEST SIDE

HISTORIC | CULTURED | SERENE

Experience the Upper West Side online

UPPER WEST SIDE
Trip Builder

TAKE YOUR PICK OF MUST-SEES AND HIDDEN GEMS

▬▬▬ The Upper West Side is a slice of old-school elegance sandwiched between Central Park and the Hudson River. Feast your eyes on lavish prewar apartment buildings, fill your culture cup at landmarks like Lincoln Center, and gorge on quintessential New York grub before unwinding in tranquil green spaces.

🗺 Neighborhood Notes

Best for Manicured parks, performing arts, casual dining and architecture.

Transport 1/2/3, B/C between Columbus Circle and 110th St stations. Note: the A and D skip from Columbus Circle to Harlem.

Getting around Explore the neighborhood on foot.

Tip Escape the corporate mega-stores on Broadway for boutique shops and local eateries on Amsterdam and Columbus.

Kick back with a beer at **Ellington in the Park** (p39) as the sun sets beyond the Hudson.
🚶 *7 min from 103rd St station*

Mosey along the spacious tree-lined promenade in **Riverside Park** (p38).
🚶 *10 min from 86th St station*

Stroll streets numbered in the **70s and 80s** (p34) to pine over prewar architecture like the Dakota.
🚶 *1 min from 72nd St station*

Hudson River

0	500 m
0	0.25 miles

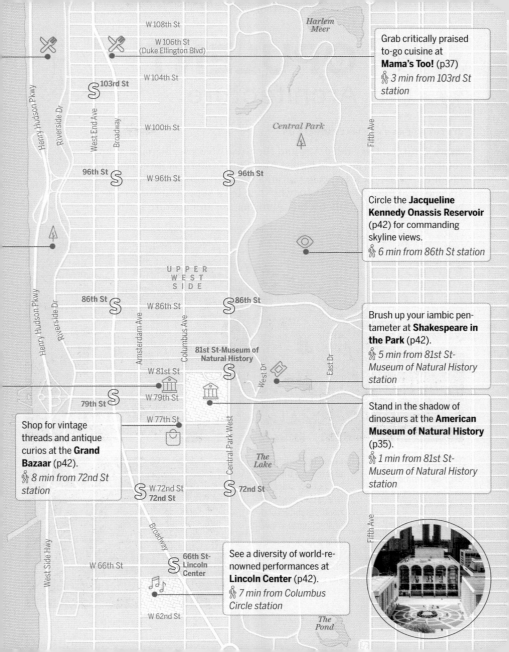

Grab critically praised to-go cuisine at **Mama's Too!** (p37)

🚶 3 min from 103rd St station

Circle the **Jacqueline Kennedy Onassis Reservoir** (p42) for commanding skyline views.

🚶 6 min from 86th St station

Brush up your iambic pentameter at **Shakespeare in the Park** (p42).

🚶 5 min from 81st St-Museum of Natural History station

Stand in the shadow of dinosaurs at the **American Museum of Natural History** (p35).

🚶 1 min from 81st St-Museum of Natural History station

Shop for vintage threads and antique curios at the **Grand Bazaar** (p42).

🚶 8 min from 72nd St station

See a diversity of world-renowned performances at **Lincoln Center** (p42).

🚶 7 min from Columbus Circle station

01 **OPULENT**
Architecture

HISTORIC | REGAL | WALKING TOUR

▬▬ Between the Gilded Age and the Great Depression, palatial apartment complexes transformed the Upper West Side from rural farmland to urban Elysium. Today, their imposing facades define the neighborhood's boulevards, attracting affluent New Yorkers who long for a slice of historic real estate. Nabbing it can cost millions, but admiring the architecture is free.

RAVENASH/SHUTTERSTOCK ©

🗺 **How To**

Getting around 1/2/3 to 72nd St station and explore on foot.

When to go Visit on a sunny morning or afternoon to view each site in all its splendor.

Look up Tourists are told to train their eyes on NYC's busy sidewalks, but to see this neighborhood's architectural stylings, gaze skywards.

Stand back Admire top-floor details like cornices and spires from the opposite side of the street.

SAMARO/GETTY IMAGES ©

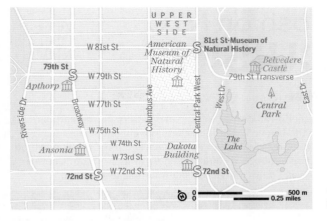

UPPER WEST SIDE

American Museum of Natural History

81st St-Museum of Natural History

W 81st St

79th St

W 79th St

Apthorp

W 77th St

Broadway

W 75th St

Ansonia

W 74th St

W 73rd St

72nd St

W 72nd St

Riverside Dr

Columbus Ave

Central Park West

West Dr

East Dr

Belvedere Castle

79th St Transverse

Central Park

Dakota Building

The Lake

72nd St

0 | 500 m
0 | 0.25 miles

Top left American Museum of Natural History **Bottom left** The Ansonia

Beaux-arts beauty Start at the extravagantly ornamented **Ansonia** (1904). In the 1970s, Bette Midler belted it out to boys at the Continental Baths, a gay bathhouse and cabaret space that once occupied the basement.

Apartment envy Read screenwriter Nora Ephron's 2006 essay 'Moving On, A Love Story' before peeking inside the wrought-iron gates of the **Apthorp** (1908) – an Italian Renaissance Revival complex she called home for 24 years.

Classic meets contemporary Walk toward Theodore Roosevelt Park to marvel at the **American Museum of Natural History**, then circle the grounds to see a hodgepodge of Gothic, Romanesque, and modern styles dating from the 1870s to present day. After admiring the exterior, step inside to see the exhibits. Everything from dinosaur fossils to recent outer-space discoveries will wow science enthusiasts.

Fairy tale in the park Head to **Belvedere Castle** (1872), a Victorian folly in Central Park with panoramic viewing platforms. Look southwest to catch a glimpse of the San Remo (1931), an art deco masterpiece with twin limestone towers.

If walls could talk Exit the park at 72nd St to see the **Dakota** (1884), a co-op so exclusive even Cher was rejected by the board. Many famous residents have cycled through this Gothic-inspired building over the past century, though none are as closely tied to the fortress as John Lennon. He was tragically murdered outside the front gates in 1980.

🏛 Europe on the Hudson

Growing up as a cellist studying at the Juilliard School and living on the Upper West Side, I was amazed by the grandeur of the prewar apartment buildings here. They looked like architecture I'd seen in Europe. I came to know them by their real names, each starting with a very serious 'The.'

Check out the Ansonia's top cupola, where a skylight was blackened during World War II as part of NYC's precautions against air raids.

By Michelle Young, founder of Untapped New York and Professor of Architecture at Columbia University, @untappedmich

02 Nosh on NYC
CUISINE

AUTHENTIC | OLD-SCHOOL | DELICIOUS

▬▬▬ You don't need a Michelin-rated meal to dine like royalty in Manhattan. This is particularly true on the Upper West Side, where the cuisine scene's main attractions come in the form of reasonably priced grab-and-go food. Chow down on these quintessential Big Apple treats, as recommended by influencer and Chelsea resident Brian Lindo, while you traipse down the sidewalk like a sovereign.

ANGELA HODSON/GETTY IMAGES ©

⫻ Multicultural Kitchens

There's nowhere else in the world where you can crave any cuisine and have access to it at your fingertips. Looking back on my most recent week alone, I've eaten Jamaican, Thai, Italian, Korean and American – and it all tasted extremely authentic.

🗺 Trip Notes

Getting here Take the 1/2/3 line to your preferred starting point between 72nd St and 103rd St stations.

When to go To avoid crowds, arrive as soon as businesses open or outside traditional meal times. Patience is otherwise mandatory for service at these popular spots.

Make it a picnic Take your treasures to nearby Riverside Park or Central Park, where benches and picnic tables abound.

By Brian Lindo, *food and lifestyle influencer,* @Briancantstopeating

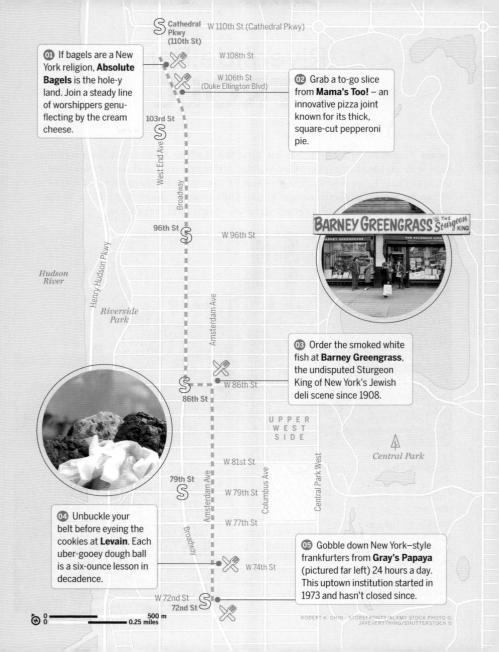

01 If bagels are a New York religion, **Absolute Bagels** is the hole-y land. Join a steady line of worshippers genuflecting by the cream cheese.

02 Grab a to-go slice from **Mama's Too!** – an innovative pizza joint known for its thick, square-cut pepperoni pie.

03 Order the smoked white fish at **Barney Greengrass**, the undisputed Sturgeon King of New York's Jewish deli scene since 1908.

04 Unbuckle your belt before eyeing the cookies at **Levain**. Each uber-gooey dough ball is a six-ounce lesson in decadence.

05 Gobble down New York–style frankfurters from **Gray's Papaya** (pictured far left) 24 hours a day. This uptown institution started in 1973 and hasn't closed since.

W 110th St (Cathedral Pkwy)
Cathedral Pkwy (110th St)
W 108th St
W 106th St (Duke Ellington Blvd)
103rd St
West End Ave
Broadway
96th St
W 96th St
Hudson River
Henry Hudson Pkwy
Riverside Park
Amsterdam Ave
W 86th St
86th St
UPPER WEST SIDE
W 81st St
Columbus Ave
Central Park West
Central Park
79th St
W 79th St
W 77th St
Broadway
Amsterdam Ave
W 74th St
W 72nd St
72nd St

0 — 500 m
0 — 0.25 miles

03 Riverside Park
STROLL

MONUMENTS | GARDENS | VIEWS

This romantic esplanade hugging the Hudson River provides a soothing escape from Manhattan's endless bustle. Although overshadowed by nearby Central Park, Riverside Park shines bright thanks to an abundance of waterfront vistas, recreational facilities and classically inspired monuments. Take to the leafy footpaths at sunset to enjoy nature's spectacular light show.

JAMES ANDREWS1/SHUTTERSTOCK ©

🗺 How To

Getting here Take the 1 to 86th St station and walk west.

When to go The park's amenities are most enjoyable between April and October.

Pick your path Ribbons of green string the park together from 59th St to 155th St, but to see its best sites, stick to the upper promenade between 89th St and 105th St.

Pedal power The riverfront thoroughfare is a relaxed place to try cycling in Manhattan. Rent a Citi Bike from one of the stations along Riverside Dr.

FELIX LIPOV/SHUTTERSTOCK ©

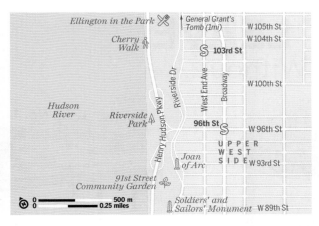

Ellington in the Park

General Grant's Tomb (1mi)

W 105th St

W 104th St

Cherry Walk

103rd St

W 100th St

Hudson River

Riverside Park

96th St

W 96th St

U P P E R
W E S T
S I D E

W 93rd St

Joan of Arc

91st Street
Community Garden

Soldiers' and
Sailors' Monument

W 89th St

500 m
0.25 miles

Top left Riverfront pathway, Riverside Park **Bottom left** Joan of Arc statue

◎ Joan of Riverside Park

The **Joan of Arc statue**, which stands regally at 93rd St, offers many opportunities for celebration and reflection. First, there's Joan herself, patron saint of France, exalted, then burned, then canonized. There is also the fact that this sculpture, dedicated in 1915, was the first statue devoted to a nonfictional woman in New York City. Fittingly, it was created by a woman – award-winning American sculptor Anna Hyatt Huntington. The statue's granite pedestal, designed by John van Pelt, incorporates limestone blocks from the Rouen tower where Joan was imprisoned before she was martyred. When we pass this statue we can honor both St Joan and the woman who forged her likeness.

By Lucie Levine, historian and writer, founder of historical tour and event company Archive on Parade, @archiveonparade

Greek inspiration Ogle the 12 Corinthian columns encircling the **Soldiers' and Sailors' Monument** (1902). The site, modeled after the Choragic monument of Lysicrates in Athens, honors Union Army members who served in the Civil War and acts as a companion piece to Grant's Tomb, located 2 miles north, the final resting place of the famed Civil War general and 18th US president.

Budding romance Between spring and autumn, friendly volunteers known as the Garden People tend to the **91st Street Community Garden** – an Edenic plot immortalized in Nora Ephron's rom-com classic *You've Got Mail*. Pause to admire the immaculate flower beds.

Full bloom Every April and May, a shock of blushing petals erupt from trees lining the **Cherry Walk** between 100th St and 125th St. Join the throngs of families relaxing underneath rose-colored blossoms.

Dinner with a view Snag an upper-level picnic table to gorge on pub grub at **Ellington in the Park**, a casual outdoor restaurant overlooking the river. Arrive before twilight to soak in the sun as it sets behind the Hudson. It's open 11am to 11pm, April through October.

DON'T LEAVE
New York Without...

01 A black-and-white cookie

Be it a bakery, a bodega, or an episode of *Seinfeld*, New York's black-and-white cookies are everywhere.

02 A 'We Are Happy to Serve You' Cup

The Anthora – a Grecian-style cardboard cup

often found in delis – has served coffee to New Yorkers since the 1960s.

03 A *New Yorker* tote

This canvas bag is the standard purse for NYC intellectuals and status symbol for word nerds.

04 Magnolia's Banana Pudding

Sex and the City put

Magnolia's cupcakes on the map but, really, it's all about the banana pudding.

05 A vintage tee from Beacon's Closet

Digging around these racks for dirt-cheap designer labels is a rite of passage for frugal fashionistas.

06 A taco from Los Tacos No. 1

Line up for an authentic Mexican taco from the stand at Chelsea Market.

07 A broken bodega umbrella

Owning a stash of cheap black umbrellas is a sign you've weathered New York like a local.

08 Superiority Burger's vegan patty

Superiority Burger is White Castle for non-meat eaters. The vegan patty is so tasty you might as well order two.

09 Clothing from your favorite NYC business

A Yankees cap. A Broadway Dance Center zip-up. Nothing says 'I Love NY' like owning merch repping your favorite local institution.

10 Junior's cheesecake

Order a slice of the best NYC-style cheesecake at the original 1950 outpost of Junior's in downtown Brooklyn.

11 A selfie framed by Manhattan Bridge

Watch out for speeding cars and aspiring influencers while snapping a selfie at Dumbo's utterly Instagrammable Water and Washington intersection.

12 Pierogi from Veselka

Veselka's Ukrainian-style pierogi have fed the tired and hungry masses on St Mark's Place since 1954.

13 A Broadway playbill

The Broadway show ends when the curtain comes down, but the iconic black-and-yellow program lasts forever.

Listings

BEST OF THE REST

 Arts & Culture

Lincoln Center

White travertine buildings dominate this modernist complex housing NYC's finest classical performances. Dress up for a night at the Metropolitan Opera, New York Philharmonic or New York City Ballet.

Shakespeare in the Park

Every summer, Central Park's open-air Delacorte Theater hosts two high-quality productions of Shakespeare's plays. Admission is free, but prepare to wait in line or win the digital TodayTix lottery for same-day seats.

Beacon Theater

Big-name headliners like Jerry Seinfeld, Radiohead and the Dalai Lama bring big crowds to the gilded interior of this former vaudeville house built in 1929.

New-York Historical Society

NYC's oldest museum, founded in 1804, houses an extensive collection of art and artifacts that examines culture and politics in New York and America. Set aside two hours to explore.

Banksy's Hammer Boy

In 2013 the owners of Zabar's placed plexiglass over this stencil spray-painted by British street artist Banksy to save it from defacement. Located around the corner from DSW on 79th St.

Food & Flea Markets

Grand Bazaar NYC

A curated collection of local artisans, chefs and antiques dealers take over an outdoor playground on Columbus Ave every Sunday to sell a mix of unique goods.

The Turnstyle Underground Market

The Columbus Circle subway station is its very own destination thanks to the 39 shops and eateries lining this subterranean mall. Grab a bite to go or take a seat to watch the commuters stream by.

Monumental Green Spaces

Riverside Park South

The rusting 69th Street Transfer Bridge is one of the few relics of a time when this riverfront promenade was filled with railroad tracks. Now, visitors wind along garden paths and clink glasses at the seasonal Pier i Cafe.

Straus Park

A tiny triangular park named after Isidor and Ida Straus, a prominent local couple who perished on the *Titanic*. Instead of escaping on a rescue boat, Ida chose to stay aboard with her husband of 41 years. A bronze statue, *Memory*, honors their devotion.

Jacqueline Kennedy Onassis Reservoir

Walk or jog clockwise on this 1.58-mile trail circling Central Park's largest body of water. Views of skyscrapers and luxury apartments appear around each bend. Cherry trees bloom along the west side in springtime.

The Ramble

Once a gay cruising site, this wooded section of Central Park now attracts birders searching for feathered friends. Visit in spring and autumn to see the plumage of migrating species.

Sheep Meadow

Thousands of New Yorkers flock to this scenic 15-acre field on Central Park's west side to picnic and sunbathe in summer.

✕🍴 Old-School Eateries

Zabar's $

Locals rub shoulders inside this gourmet grocer known for smoked fish, rugelach, artisanal cheeses and bagels. Grab your goods to go, and eat in nearby Riverside Park.

Cafe Luxembourg $$$

Upper-crust clientele started knocking back cocktails in the 1980s at this French bistro near Lincoln Center. Slide into a red-leather booth and enjoy the ambience while nibbling on steak frites.

Old John's Diner $$

This luncheonette near Lincoln Center retains its original 1950s charm. Order the kids a classic egg cream and have yourself a Manhattan. Sit bar-side for a soda-shop experience.

🍸 Casual Cuisine & Cocktails

Báhn Vietnamese Shop House $$

A bright and cheery restaurant serving homestyle Vietnamese dishes so authentic you'll think you're in Hanoi. Spring rolls, sticky rice cakes and the assortment of banh mi are fan favorites.

Chick Chick $$

Korean- and Nashville-inspired chicken sandwiches rule this low-key poultry palace, while dishes like kimchi fried rice and ramen round out the cross-cultural menu. Ideal for a quick meal or dinner to-go.

Daily Provisions $

Danny Meyer's sunny all-day cafe famous for BECs, BLTs and baked goods. Visit first thing in the morning to get a cruller – the doughnut's French cousin – before they're gone.

Jacob's Pickles $$

Rowdy brunch and dinner spot for creative Southern comfort food. Try a flight of pickles and add bacon to one of the 20 craft beers on tap.

Peacefood Cafe $$

Vegans rejoice over the eclectic offerings at this plant-based restaurant, which include everything from juices and grain bowls to burgers and baked goods.

El Mitote $$

Guadalajara-style street food and classic Mexican platters served on colorful trays in a convivial space. Look up 'Los 41 maricones' for insight into the LGBT-inspired mural painted inside.

Nobody Told Me $$

Trendy cocktail bar frequented by the 20s and 30s crowd for crafty mix drinks and chef-driven pub fare. Great for laid-back date nights or catching up with friends.

📖 Books & Boutiques

Magpie

A quirky boutique for stationery, gifts and homegoods. The ecofriendly items are largely locally made, fair trade or crafted from sustainable materials.

Shakespeare and Co

Uptown intellectuals cram into this indie bookshop's cafe to devour the latest bestsellers while sipping on espresso. Don't fret if you can't find a title – an on-site machine prints manuscripts within minutes.

 Scan to find more things to do on the Upper West Side online

04 A Central Park
PICNIC

NATURE | RECREATION | DINING

Central Park's 843 acres of meadows, gardens, forests and lakes might be the antidote to concrete-jungle chaos, but finding tranquility is tricky if you stick to the well-worn paths below 72nd St. Seek out solitude while picnicking along the weeping-willow waterfront of the Pool – an uptown Arcadia more like the Adirondacks than the heart of Manhattan.

WINSTON TAN/SHUTTERSTOCK ©

🗺 How To

Getting here Take the B/C line to 103rd St station. From there, enter the park at 100th St or 103rd St.

When to go Eating alfresco on sunny days between April and October. The trails near the Pool are pleasurable year-round.

When nature calls Find public restrooms on the Great Hill near 105th St.

Deep dive Download the Bloomberg Connects app for a free audioguide to Central Park.

MARTIN CLOUTIER/SHUTTERSTOCK ©

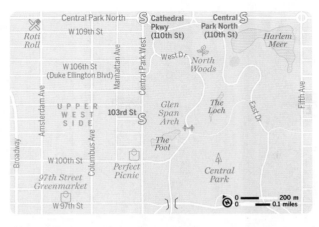

Find your food Peek inside **Perfect Picnic** on Central Park West to find park essentials like blankets, baskets and lunch grub. On Fridays, forage for locally grown produce, handmade cheese and artisanal bread at the **97th Street Greenmarket**. Whole Foods is a reliable stop for picnic-friendly fare, as are casual neighborhood restaurants like **Roti Roll**, which sells Indian street snacks.

Pick a spot Picnickers usually commune in the sun-drenched meadows around the Pool, but if you want something private, head to the rocky grove hidden along the northern banks. If you require a seat, stick to the south side and claim the stand-alone wood bench framed by bald-cypress trees.

Meet the neighbors Central Park's northwest corner is first-class real estate for wildlife. Mallard ducks preside over the Pool while gray squirrels and chipmunks reign among the woodlands. On sunny days, turtles catch rays on rocky outcroppings, and raccoons scamper around the treetops at twilight. Keep an eye out for red-tailed hawks, cardinals and blue jays, many of which nest on overhead branches.

Take a hike Once you're satiated, follow the Pool's eastern path as it pours down a 20ft cascade and rushes underneath the rustic **Glen Span Arch**. This stream, known as the Loch, swerves through the **North Woods** – a 40-acre forest – and feeds the Harlem Meer, an idyllic lake near 110th St.

Top left Central Park
Bottom left Squirrel, Central Park

⁓⁓ Water from the Source

The Pool and its connecting waterways were inspired by Montayne's Rivulet – a natural stream originating at present-day Columbus Ave and 95th St. Still, this area is far from organic. A 48in pipe masterfully hidden near the Pool's southern grotto combines the stream with city water, bringing designers Calvert Vaux and Frederick Law Olmsted's vision to life.

MIDTOWN

CULTURE | MUSIC | THEATER

Experience
Midtown
online

MIDTOWN
Trip Builder

TAKE YOUR PICK OF MUST-SEES AND HIDDEN GEMS

▬▬▬ Midtown has it all – round-the-clock entertainment in Times Square, the majesty of the Empire State Building, cheerful Broadway musicals, incredible restaurants, bustling crowds and so much more. It is New York City at its most energetic and alive. Read on to experience its greatest highlights and unique corners.

🗺 Neighborhood Notes

Best for A fun night out, sky-high views, delicious dining.

Transport A/C/E, N/Q/R/W, S, 1/2/3, 7 lines.

Getting around The best way to get around in Midtown is on foot.

Foot traffic Seventh and Eighth Aves around Times Square can get packed; take Sixth Ave or Ninth Ave for faster foot travel.

500 m
0.25 miles

Gaze at the vast permanent collections and modern architecture of the **Museum of Modern Art** (p54).
🚶 5 min from Fifth Ave/53rd St station

Catch a musical on the iconic **Broadway** (p50) theater strip.
🚶 5 min from Times Sq-42nd St station

Enjoy the hustle-bustle and all-night lights of the epic **Times Square**.
🚶 1 min from Times Sq-42nd St station

Visit the towering **Empire State Building** (p58) on the always-glamorous Fifth Ave.
🚶 8 min from 34th St-Herald Sq station

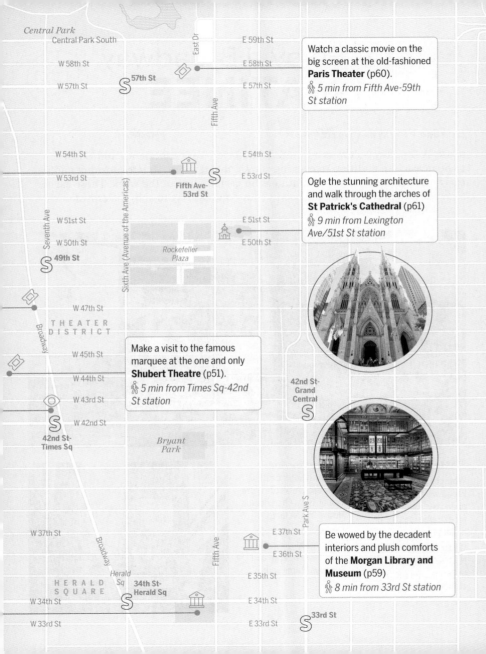

Central Park

Central Park South

W 58th St

W 57th St

57th St

E 59th St

E 58th St

E 57th St

Watch a classic movie on the big screen at the old-fashioned **Paris Theater** (p60).

🚶 *5 min from Fifth Ave-59th St station*

W 54th St

W 53rd St

Fifth Ave-53rd St

E 54th St

E 53rd St

Ogle the stunning architecture and walk through the arches of **St Patrick's Cathedral** (p61)

🚶 *9 min from Lexington Ave/51st St station*

W 51st St

W 50th St

49th St

E 51st St

E 50th St

Rockefeller Plaza

W 47th St

THEATER DISTRICT

W 45th St

Make a visit to the famous marquee at the one and only **Shubert Theatre** (p51).

🚶 *5 min from Times Sq-42nd St station*

W 44th St

W 43rd St

W 42nd St

42nd St-Times Sq

Bryant Park

42nd St-Grand Central

W 37th St

Herald Sq

HERALD SQUARE

34th St-Herald Sq

W 34th St

W 33rd St

E 37th St

E 36th St

E 35th St

E 34th St

E 33rd St

33rd St

Be wowed by the decadent interiors and plush comforts of the **Morgan Library and Museum** (p59)

🚶 *8 min from 33rd St station*

05

Enjoy a Broadway
MATINEE

CULTURE | THEATER | MUSIC

A Broadway show is a quintessential New York experience and is not to be missed. In addition to evening shows, theaters put on late-morning and early-afternoon shows called matinees on certain days of the week. These earlier shows are sometimes not at capacity, so it's a great way to skip the crowds!

MURAT CAN KIRMIZIGUL/SHUTTERSTOCK ©

📖 How To

When to go The Broadway theaters are open year-round, except for extreme reasons or holidays.

Getting here A/C/E, N/Q/R/W, S, 1/2/3, 7 to Times Sq-42nd St station.

What to wear Put on your theater best! Matinees are a little more casual, but a sharp look is always appreciated.

Timing tip Matinees are on Wednesdays and Saturdays 10am–2pm and Sundays 11am–3pm.

RICHARD LEVINE/ALAMY STOCK PHOTO ©

Top left Theatre billboards, Times Square **Bottom left** Hudson Theatre

Top Five Theaters

Shubert Theatre Though the Lyceum Theater is the oldest continually operating theater on Broadway, the Shubert arguably has the most classical look. Its iconic light-bulb marquee has always embodied Broadway and its rich history.

Hudson Theatre Newly refurbished and re-opened as a Broadway house in 2017, the Hudson boasts modern seating and expanded women's restrooms – something most of the other historic houses on Broadway are lacking, hence the lines at intermission. The Hudson also serves beverages at the bar in real glassware that you can take back to your seat – a simple, elegant touch that hopefully will continue.

Helen Hayes Theatre The smallest Broadway house at under 600 seats, this theater is a truly intimate space where it's difficult to find a bad seat for both plays and musicals alike.

Studio 54 This Roundabout Theatre Company–owned house is located on the former site of the world-famous disco-era nightclub of the same name. That history alone is enough to make it memorable.

Vivian Beaumont Theater The one Broadway house located further uptown; Lincoln Center's Vivian Beaumont is a wonderfully large three-quarter-thrust stage that truly brings the drama to the audience. The unique bonus is that Lincoln Center is itself a beautiful shrine to the arts with a gorgeous plaza that features live performances and events.

Insider Ticket Tip

For same-day discount tickets to Broadway and Off-Broadway shows, visit the Times Square **TKTS booth** (additional locations are at Lincoln Center and South Street Seaport), and then climb the booth's red steps for a view of the Times Square billboards and lights. The central area is home to the famous MTV Studios and the biggest LED display in the world; both are must-sees. If you're tired of the crowds and rude mascot characters, Rockefeller Center is to the east and Hell's Kitchen to the west, and each area has shops and dining galore. Alternatively, take in Times Square at 3am when it's just you, the bright lights and the statue of entertainer George M Cohan.

Recommended by Gregory Jacobs-Roseman, *musical theater composer, lyricist and producer, @GJRoseman, gregjr.com*

MIDTOWN EXPERIENCES

Broadway History

SEAN PAVONE/SHUTTERSTOCK ©

BEHIND EVERY MARQUEE THERE IS A STORY
The history of theater in New York is as one would expect it to be – a dramatic roller coaster of highs, lows, ups, downs and excitement. Whether offering Shakespearian plays in the 1700s or the bright lights and glamour of today's Times Square, the New York theater scene is always in style.

Theater has been part of New York City's soul since its earliest origins, but the remarkable spectacle that is 'Broadway' as the world knows and loves it today took time to grow and develop. It is a theatrical world that has been consistently active, slowing only briefly for monumental events such as the Revolutionary War in the late 18th century, the Great Depression and the Covid-19 pandemic.

The first large theater to open in New York City was established by Walter Murray and Thomas Kean in 1750. The mainstay performances were classical in nature, focusing on operatic theater and Shakespearian plays. The most popular form of performance, the ballad opera, originated in the 18th century and featured comic plots with music interspersed between the actors' dialogue. One of the earliest and most renowned plays in the genre was *The Beggar's Opera* (1728), by John Gay, which would set the tone for all of its successors. The ballad opera is now considered the precursor to the musical as the world thinks of it today.

In New York, after the Revolutionary War, the 2000-seat Park Theatre was built to massive success, followed soon after by the Bowery Theater in 1826. Niblo's Garden, located at Broadway and Prince St, became a popular location and thus became the heart of 'Broadway,' and so theater got its moniker. Originally, Broadway theater was unique to downtown Manhattan – it was only in the early 1900s that it moved to Times Square, where it has remained since. The Broadway District as it is known today is located from W 41st St to W 53rd St between Sixth and Ninth

Left 42nd St **Middle** Tony Award
Right New York City Center

Aves. In order for a play to be considered Broadway, it must be held within one of the 41 designated professional theaters with 500 or more seats found within these street borders.

The 1920s was the decade that gave rise to a new style of American play. For the first time, John O'Neill, a writer of original plays sans music, began to show that dramatic writing had a place on the Broadway stage. His work, like the iconic *Behind the Horizon,* paved the way for music-free greats such as Tennessee Williams and Arthur Miller to stake their Broadway claims. The 1930s saw a slump with the Great Depression, but Broadway bounced back full force. The Musical Theater Repertoire, as it is known today, was built from 1950 to 1970 with the creation of plays such as the incomparable *Guys and Dolls* and *My Fair Lady*.

> Originally, Broadway theater was unique to downtown Manhattan – it was only in the early 1900s that it moved to Times Square, where it has remained since.

The famous musical *Little Johnny Jones* features the lyric, 'Give my regards to Broadway!' And, rightfully so, as Broadway remains one of the most valuable and important industries in New York City. In 2012 ticket sales totaled $1 billion and over 12 million people attended plays. The Tony Awards, the 'Oscars' of the theater world, began in 1947 with 11 categories and continues to be celebrated every year at Radio City Music Hall in Midtown, just a few minutes from the Theater District.

🎭 Off-Broadway Highlights

Broadway certainly isn't the only option for theater in the Theater District. Some of the most interesting and exciting theater is happening in the smaller venues around Times Square. New World Stages, Theater Row, Playwright's Horizons, New York City Center – these are just a few of the Off-Broadway houses and companies worth exploring. Some of the best and brightest actors, musicians, producers and directors in the world participate in hundreds of Off-Broadway shows annually. Academy and Tony Award nominees and winners often put their secret passion projects onto the Off-Broadway stages. Don't miss out!

06 MoMA Sculpture GARDEN

ART | CULTURE | MUSEUMS

The Museum of Modern Art is internationally recognized as one of the most significant modern-art museums in the world. In addition to its vast collections, hidden inside is yet another treasure – a picturesque outdoor sculpture garden that is one of the most unique places in New York City.

KUMAR SRISKANDAN/ALAMY STOCK PHOTO ©

How To

When to go Spring, summer and fall are prime times for this experience. The garden is sometimes closed during the winter months.

Getting here F to 57th St station, B/D/E to Seventh Ave station.

What to wear The museum is vast and will require lots of walking, so sneakers are best. For events, feel free to bring your heels.

Ticket pricing Adults ($25), seniors and persons with a disability ($18), students ($14), children (free).

ELIZABETH WAKE/ALAMY STOCK PHOTO ©

The Secret Garden

Officially named the Abby Aldrich Rockefeller Sculpture Garden, this delightful urban green space is a secret favorite of many New Yorkers. The unexpected coziness of the garden is what conjures up its charm. The design is extremely intentional, and MoMA has described the architect's vision of creating a 'roofless room' to make the garden as comfortable as your home. It opened in 1939, then was redesigned in 1953 by Philip Johnson. The floors are paved with gorgeous marble, and there are four separate areas all overflowing with plant beds, fountains, small pools and many tree varieties. The garden is meant to be a forum for relaxation and self-expression, and music performances, events and protests have all occurred here.

The pièce de résistance is, of course, the sculptures. The sculptures on display rotate

CHOONGKY/SHUTTERSTOCK ©

🐦 Bird-Watching in the Garden

The sculpture garden is so verdant that many birds come and visit to sing or take a bath in the fountains. If you're visiting in the springtime, be sure to ask a staff member about the many bird varieties you might see on the grounds.

Above left, above right and left
MoMA Sculpture Garden

to keep the space lively and fresh, but their creators represent a who's who of modern art. Henri Matisse, Pablo Picasso, Rachel Whiteread, Barnett Newman, Hector Guimard and Aristide Maillol have all been on display alongside the smooth pathways and bubbling fountains. Tables, chairs and benches are scattered throughout for meeting and chatting about the art with friends, or simply enjoying a meditative time alone with the artworks on display. A fun fact – and a testament to the garden's penchant for unique creative offerings – is that the first-ever synth concert took place in this garden on August 28, 1969. The museum was the very first to introduce the synthesizer as an instrument, and thus the course of music history was forever changed.

Arguably, the most beautiful piece in the garden is the statue inspired by the Narcissus and Echo myth in Greek mythology. As the story goes, Narcissus was a mortal of

📍 Favorite Activities Near MoMA

Walk uptown from MoMA to enjoy a stroll through Central Park, which is always perfection. The 59th St entrance is really nearby. If you're walking downtown **Bryant Park**, on 42nd St and Fifth Ave, is also excellent. Watch outdoor movies here. **Del Frisco's** is a great classic New American restaurant with a perfect view of the rink at Rockefeller Center.

And, speaking of dining, try **Havana Central**. It has an unassuming, bustling atmosphere and phenomenal food. Try the mojitos!

Recommended by Nadia Salim, *artist and MoMA Design Store staff,* *@astro_knowme*

Far left Del Frisco's **Near left** Bryant Park **Below** MoMA Design Store

such beauty that it was almost divine. He had an admirer in Echo, a forest nymph, but he cruelly rejected her as he loved no one but himself. The sculpture is placed directly above a reflecting pool where one can watch Narcissus gaze at his own reflection adoringly. Be sure to throw a coin into the fountain, as many do, and make a wish!

Shopping the Modern Way

A lesser-known attraction at the Museum of Modern Art is the must-see **MoMA Design Store**. This store, 100% inspired by the modern art in the museum's collections, offers signature items such as furniture for home and office; accessories such as eyewear, apparel, umbrellas and watches; and even technology such as cameras and specialty headphones. The Design Store is curated as meticulously as the museum itself, and even if one doesn't buy anything, it is impossible not to be swept away by the quality and aesthetic of the store. It has one location in Midtown at the main museum site, and a sister store in SoHo on Spring St.

07 Empire State SUNRISE

CULTURE | ARCHITECTURE | BUILDINGS

The Empire State Building embodies everything that New York represents – culture, style, ambition and the idea that this city can make your wildest dreams come true. Wherever one hails from, watching from the 86th floor as the sun rises over Manhattan's iconic gleaming skyline is the ultimate source of inspiration.

ANGELA WEISS/AFP/GETTY IMAGES ©

🗺 How To

When to go This iconic building is open year-round.

Getting here B/D/F/M, N/Q/R/W to 34th St-Herald Sq station.

What to wear Casual wear and sneakers are the best choice for this experience.

Tip If you have a smart-phone, take a photo using the panoramic feature. The 360-degree sunrise view from the 86th floor is worth capturing!

JOAQUIN OSSORIO CASTILLO/SHUTTERSTOCK ©

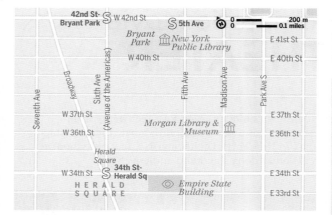

42nd St-
Bryant Park · W 42nd St · 5th Ave · 0 / 0 · 200 m / 0.1 miles

Bryant Park · New York Public Library · E 41st St

W 40th St · E 40th St

Broadway · Seventh Ave · Sixth Ave (Avenue of the Americas) · Fifth Ave · Madison Ave · Park Ave S

W 37th St · E 37th St

W 36th St · Morgan Library & Museum · E 36th St

Herald Square

W 34th St · 34th St-Herald Sq · E 34th St

HERALD SQUARE · Empire State Building · E 33rd St

Top left View from Empire State Building at sunrise **Bottom left** Aluminum relief, Empire State Building lobby

Empire State of Mind

At a towering 102 stories, the Empire State Building is one of the most distinctive buildings in the world. Its unique art deco finish gives it a crystalline quality that reflects light to perfection. Built from 1930 to 1931, it was designed by Shreve, Lamb & Harmon and is located on Fifth Ave between 33rd and 34th Sts. The quintessential symbol of New York City, it has even been named one of the Seven Wonders of the Modern World by the American Society of Civil Engineers.

NYC from on High

The most popular tour is the daytime tour of the 86th floor's Main Deck, but the sleeper hit is the unforgettable experience of watching the sun rise over the city. This tour is limited to just 40 visitors, making it a low-key, intimate experience at which to enjoy a cup of coffee, take some photos and savor a meditative moment. To the north, you'll see the rest of Midtown, all the way up to Central Park and beyond. To the west, you're reminded that Manhattan is an island when you see the rolling Hudson River streaming by. And, of course, to the south you will see the quaint architecture of downtown – a stark contrast against the towering One World Trade Center, which marks the end of the island at South Street Seaport. This experience is New York City at its finest.

🏛 Morgan Library & Museum

The Morgan Library and Museum is truly a sight to behold. It was founded by New York's legendary financier and mercantile magnate JP Morgan as his personal library and later turned into a public repository. It is both a library and a museum, with on-site historic manuscripts and rare books in addition to drawings, paintings and prints from the old masters. The Morgan Library and Museum is a 15-minute walk from the **New York Public Library**, so comparing and contrasting these equally opulent spaces is worth the time. The New York Public Library is known for its stunning and ornate marble facade, the two massive stone lions in its courtyard, and its decadent interior. The main reading room is the stuff of fantasy with dimly lit lamps, long ornate wooden tables for studying, and ornate gold and brass detailing that extends to everything from doorknobs to light switches.

08 A Historic Movie **THEATER**

CULTURE | ART | CINEMA

The Paris Theater is Midtown's hidden treat. Rest feet weary from walking the city and take a seat in this quaint, landmark movie theater, which is the oldest art-house cinema in New York. The theater is a real old-school gem, with only one screen, a small concessions stand and endless charm.

SEE NETFLIX'S 17 OSCAR®-NOMINATED FILMS

CRIP CAMP   DA 5 BLOODS   EuroVision   HILLBILLY ELEGY   If anything happens I love you   the life ahead

A Love Song For Latasha   MA RAINEY'S BLACK BOTTOM   Mank   THE MIDNIGHT   MY OCTOPUS

PATTI MCCONVILLE/ALAMY STOCK PHOTO ©

🗺 How To

When to go This movie theater is open year-round.

Getting here N/R/W to Fifth Ave/59th St station.

What to wear The movie theater is casual and surrounding areas may require a lot of walking; wear sneakers!

Check the listings Be sure to peruse the website's calendar before visiting. Sometimes directors and actors stop in for a Q&A.

GABRIELPEVIDE/GETTY IMAGES ©

Top left Paris Theater **Bottom left** St Patrick's Cathedral

Paris, NYC

Paris Theater opened on September 13, 1948, and was built by a French distributor named Pathé as a place to screen his films. It's an extremely well-appointed theater with only one screen in front of 571 beautifully upholstered seats. Its unique style and central location made it a hit, and it quickly became a top screening location for some of the finest films in the world. The theater has endured its share of financial difficulties, as New York City and the world has undergone economic ups and downs. But, on November 6, 2019, mega-producers Netflix revived the theater and are now in charge of all of its screenings and programming. Under Netflix's leadership it is now home to excellent exclusives, retrospectives, premieres and other events. Filmmakers and actors are often called in for Q&As to discuss their work, and with Netflix at the helm, the roster is often 100% A-listers.

Northern Midtown

The theater is also surrounded by the best of the best of northern Midtown. Central Park, the Plaza Hotel, the Museum of Modern Art (MoMA), St Patrick's Cathedral, Rockefeller Center, the New York Public Library and Radio City Music Hall are all within short walking distance. This is the perfect place at which to kick back and enjoy a moment of rest before continuing your journey through bustling Midtown.

St Patrick's Cathedral

A very short walk from the Paris Theater is one of Midtown's best known and beloved attractions, St Patrick's Cathedral. The church is absolutely massive – a beautiful Gothic old-world masterpiece, which almost seems out of place among the modern skyscrapers surrounding it. Entering the church is a solemn experience, with thousands of tourists speaking in hushed tones and awed by the enormous limestone arches and gilded altars. The best-kept secret is the stunning shrine to the Virgin Mary in the back, complete with a marble sculpture of the *Pietà* to the right of its entrance.

Listings

BEST OF THE REST

🍴 Pre- & Post-Theater Eats

Joe Allen $$$

The famous watering hole for the theatrically inclined, Joe Allen's is a historic institution. Note the humorous posters of Broadway flops adorning the walls.

Becco $$$

On W 46th St's 'Restaurant Row,' Becco is touristy, but that's easy to overlook due to its signature item: three unlimited, daily pasta preparations served table-side.

West Bank Cafe $$

This wonderful American cafe on 42nd St is a Hell's Kitchen staple with wonderful cocktails, food and live music. The truffled mac 'n' cheese is particularly heavenly.

Osteria al Doge $$$

Specializing in Venetian cuisine, Osteria al Doge has a warm atmosphere and is perfect for a quick meal at the bar or a full meal at a table. Definitely try a risotto!

Blue Dog Cookhouse & Bar $$

This is a wonderful spot for a hand-crafted cocktail at the bar before the theater or for its excellent dinner menu. It also serves a killer brunch.

Quality Bistro $$$

This upscale French eatery is perfect if you have a date or in-law to impress. It's close to the theaters and has all of the classics.

La Masseria NY $$$

A Theater District classic that serves hearty Southern Italian fare in a down-home old-world environment. The service is impeccable.

Pure Thai Cookhouse $$

This casual no-nonsense eatery is great for a quick and tasty bite. Don't be fooled by its humble bearings: it's often rated the best Thai food in the city.

Rex Coffee $

Rex has served ridiculously good coffee and sandwiches since 2013. Arrive before it closes in the afternoon. The egg sandwiches are divine.

Jolly Goat Coffee Bar $

A delightful coffeehouse offering strong espresso drinks and teas. It's cozy and offers a variety of baked goods.

Frisson Espresso $

Sample the rich espresso drinks at this bright and cozy coffee shop. Pastries, sweets and some light lunch fare are also available.

Amy's Bread $

For those seeking a sweet treat after lunch, this award-winning bakery has all of your dessert needs covered. Its layer cakes, in particular, are delicious.

Amy's Bread

🍸 Pre- & Post-Theater Cocktails

Casellula $$$

This Hell's Kitchen cheese-focused wine bar and restaurant is wonderful for pre- or post-theater wine. Order the Fromagère's Choice for a selection curated by its cheese experts.

Hurley's Saloon $

This Irish pub and restaurant is a warm neighborhood hangout with friendly bartenders and tasty pub food. The restaurant features multiple levels and a rooftop garden.

Glass House Tavern $$

A bistro that's a great spot for pre-theater dinner and a favorite for after-show drinks.

Russian Vodka Room $$$

This windowless gem of a bar features a huge selection of infused vodkas and Russian delights. Visit *after* the theater or you might not remember the play!

Lillie's Victorian Establishment $$

Stop in for a drink and try one of the many options on the gin-and-tonics menu at this 49th St bar and restaurant that harkens back to Dickensian London.

Rum House (in the Hotel Edison) $$

A swanky hotel cocktail bar, the Rum House has a fantastic assortment of rum delights and a gorgeous wood-paneled bar. Perfect for a tasty nightcap.

Bar Centrale $$$

This chic bar in a town house without a sign is a prime spot for celebrity sightings. Make a reservation online at least a week in advance.

Aldo Sohm Wine Bar $$$

An upscale-casual wine bar, Aldo Sohm has cozy couch seating and a nice variety of gourmet small plates. Offerings include tasty duck confit lettuce wraps.

Manhattan cocktail

🎵 Cabaret! Cabaret!

Feinstein's/54 Below

'Broadway's Supper Club' is one of the premier music and cabaret venues in New York. Here you can watch the best performers and writers of Broadway and beyond.

Don't Tell Mama

This famous piano bar and cabaret has a performing staff and an open mike. Listen to show tunes into the wee hours of the morning, or put your name in to perform one yourself!

Laurie Beechman Theatre

Even if you don't have theater plans, this local winner hosts live cabaret, music, comedy and variety shows throughout the week.

📖 Theater Bookshops

The Drama Book Shop

This 104-year-old diamond full of songbooks, libretti, scores, coffee and snacks almost closed, but was purchased and saved by a group of devotees, including *Hamilton* writer Lin-Manuel Miranda.

 Scan to find more things to do in Midtown online

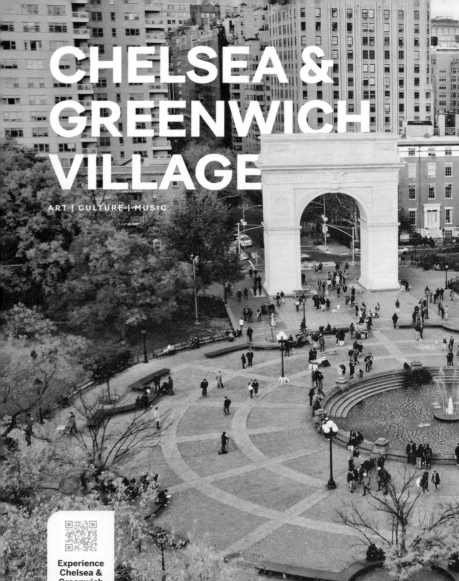

CHELSEA & GREENWICH VILLAGE

ART | CULTURE | MUSIC

Experience
Chelsea &
Greenwich
Village
online

CHELSEA & GREEN- WICH VILLAGE
Trip Builder

TAKE YOUR PICK OF MUST-SEES AND HIDDEN GEMS

Chelsea and Greenwich Village are two of the most eclectic neighborhoods in New York City. Home to iconic artists ranging from John Lennon to Carrie Bradshaw herself, Sarah Jessica Parker, they're also home to the city's largest LGBTIQ+ community and its premier art-gallery destination. What's not to love?

🗺 Neighborhood Notes

Best for A night out, delicious dining, gorgeous green spaces, art.

Transport A/C/E, L to 14th St/Eighth Ave station, C/E to 23rd St/Eighth Ave station.

Getting around This area is best explored on foot or by bike.

Tip The border between the West Village and Chelsea is 14th St.

0
0
500 m
0.25 miles

Eleventh Ave

The High Line

W 24th St

W 24th St

W 23rd St

Hudson River Park

See the finest in multicultural and African American fine art at **Jack Shainman Gallery** (p71).
🚶 *10 min from 23rd St/ Eighth Ave station*

Eleventh Ave (West Side Hwy)

Tenth Ave

W 16th St

W 15th St

W 14th St

The High Line

Washington St

Little Island

Hudson River

Stroll through an urban garden paradise at the **High Line** (p70).
🚶 *9 min from 14th St/ Eighth Ave station*

West Side Hwy

Hudson River Park

W 28th St

S 28th St

W 27th St

Explore fashion history at the **Museum at Fashion Institute of Technology** (p76)
🚶 5 min from 23rd St/Seventh Ave station

W 26th St

23rd St
S

Savor the mind-blowing cupcakes at **Billy's Bakery** (p84) on Ninth Ave.
🚶 9 min from 23rd St/Eighth Ave station

W 22nd St

W 21st St

CHELSEA

Admire the architecture and tree-lined beauty of **Bank St** (p69).
🚶 7 min from Christopher St station

UNION SQUARE

Gansevoort St

Greenwich St

Hudson St

Eighth Ave

Bank St

Grab drinks at **Stonewall Inn** (p75) the birthplace of the LGBTIQ+ rights movement.
🚶 1 min from Christopher St station

Visit New York's top downtown people-watching destination – **Washington Square Park** (p84).
🚶 1 min from Christopher St station

W 8th St

Seventh Ave

W 4th St

W 10th St

Christopher St

Christopher St-Sheridan Sq

Waverly Pl

Washington Sq N

Washington Sq E

Sing along with friends to popular show tunes and more at **Marie's Crisis** (p74).
🚶 1 min from Christopher St station

Grove St

Sheridan Sq

Washington Pl

Bleecker St

W 4th St

Washington Sq S

Washington Sq W

S
W 4th St-Washington Sq

09 Hudson River Park
SUNSET

NATURE | PARKS | GREEN SPACES

Hudson River Park is the ultimate downtown oasis for West Side New Yorkers. Spanning 4 miles along the Hudson River, it's the perfect place for a casual picnic or jog, or excellent water views. The tasty wineries and oyster bars sprinkled along the boardwalk are also well worth a visit.

LAZYLLAMA/SHUTTERSTOCK ©

🗺 How To

Getting here A/C/E, L to 14th St/Eighth Ave station; walk west to the river.

When to go Spring, summer and fall are prime times for this experience.

What to wear This area is full of cobblestones and boardwalks; wear sneakers.

Tip Check the appropriate websites for information on when the sun is going to set so you can set up your location.

JAMES ANDREWS1/SHUTTERSTOCK ©

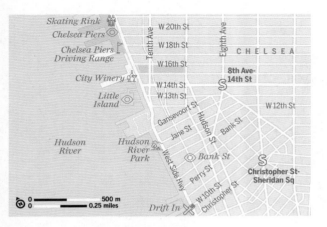

A Perfect Day, Capped with a Sunset

Greenwich Village is one of the finest places in all of New York City for a good old-fashioned neighborhood stroll. The 19th-century architecture, quaint and quiet tree-lined streets, and interesting history make for a deeply peaceful experience. **Bank St** is one of the prettiest streets in the neighborhood – once home to John Lennon, Yoko Ono and Sid Vicious, it is the ultimate picturesque cobblestoned classic, with buildings dating back to 1798. The Hudson River Park waterfront is particularly flawless at sunset, and you won't regret planning your day around a sparkling crimson-sunset ending.

If you choose to start your journey further north in the streets of Chelsea (15th to 29th Sts), walk all the way west to the waterfront and become acquainted with the famous **Chelsea Piers**. This boardwalk is home to a cornucopia of riverside entertainment, including the **Chelsea Piers Driving Range**, where you can sign up for a golf lesson, or the family-friendly **Skating Rink**, which operates year-round. Stop in for pre- or post-sunset appetizers, cocktails, drinks, dinner or picnic take-out at wonderful restaurants such as **Drift In**, **Grand Banks**, **Hudson Clearwater** or **City Winery**.

Top left Hudson River Park
Bottom left Little Island

🏛 Little Island

This urban green space located within the larger Hudson River Park is unlike any other area of the city. Standing within the Hudson River itself, its remarkable exterior is made of 132 massive concrete 'tulips' that emerge from the water to form the grounds of the park. It's a true feat of engineering as each 'tulip' has a different weight load to support the soil, trees, lawns and flower beds. The original piles from Pier 54 are still lodged in the river, allowing the park to disturb aquatic life as little as possible.

10

HIGH LINE
& Whitney Museum

ART | CULTURE | PARKS

One of the smaller enclaves within the larger neighborhoods of Greenwich Village and Chelsea is the glamorous Meatpacking District. The High Line starts in this area and stretches up into Chelsea. The Whitney Museum of American Art is one of its top attractions.

FRANÇOIS ROUX/SHUTTERSTOCK ©

🗺 How To

When to go Spring, summer and fall are prime times for the High Line. The Whitney Museum is a great place to visit in all four seasons.

Getting here A/C/E, L to 14th St/Eighth Ave station.

Tip The Whitney Museum is free on Fridays from 7pm to 9:30pm.

Avoid the crowds Visit the High Line and the Whitney Museum on weekdays.

RBLFMR/SHUTTERSTOCK ©

High Line Highlights

With over 15 unique planting zones and 110,000 plants, this vibrant urban park in downtown Manhattan is a sight to behold. Built on a historic, elevated rail line, it's more than just a park or beautiful green space. Local and national art installations, performances, an amazing variety of gourmet foods and dining stations, and a delightfully communal atmosphere greet you with every visit. Once an overgrown, abandoned railway, the city took it over as a way to promote sustainability initiatives and give the unique city landmark back to New Yorkers. View the streets of the Meatpacking District and Chelsea from up above with a walk through this 'highway in the sky!'

EQROY/SHUTTERSTOCK ©

🖼 Jack Shainman Gallery

This gallery has robust programming and two well-organized Chelsea locations, and is home to top artists such as Kerry James Marshall, Nick Cave, Carrie Mae Weems and Hank Willis Thomas. It's celebrated for its multicultural range of artists and for championing emerging talent.

Above left High Line **Above right** View of the High Line from street level at Chelsea Market **Left** Whitney Museum of American Art

Beneath the northern end of the High Line, you can find the famous art galleries of Chelsea, which are open most weekdays and weekends. Here a front-row seat to cutting-edge modern and contemporary art is on offer. Be sure to check gallery listings to see if you can attend an evening opening, which are free to the public and sometimes serve sparkling wine or champagne to attendees.

Whitney – Museum of American Dreams

Designed by renowned architect Renzo Piano and elegantly placed between the High Line and the Hudson River, the Whitney Museum of American Art is a must-see art extravaganza. Its collections are unique in that they are solely devoted to the art of the United States. What also makes this museum interesting is its focus on artists who are still alive,

Chelsea Gallery Shortlist

Gagosian Gallery Almost like a museum, this gallery is indisputably excellent and has sister locations worldwide.

David Zwirner Gallery This space is home to greats like Yayoi Kusama, but sometimes has long lines. Visit on a weekday.

Paula Cooper Gallery Paula Cooper opened the first-ever gallery in SoHo, then moved in 1996 to this stellar Chelsea location.

Lisson Gallery This gallery located under the High Line opened in 2016 and has an amazing 4500 sq ft of space.

Tanya Bonakdar Gallery For those who prefer more interactive art, this gallery offers installation and sculptural pieces.

Gagosian Gallery
Paula Cooper Gallery
W 26th St
CHELSEA
W 24th St
W 24th St
Lisson Gallery
23rd St
W 23rd St
Hudson River Park
Tanya Bonakdar Gallery
W 21st St
David Zwirner Gallery
Tenth Ave
Ninth Ave
Eighth Ave
Eleventh Ave (West Side Hwy)
High Line
The High Line
8th Ave-14th St
Hudson River
W 14th St
Little Island
Gansevoort St
Whitney Museum of American Art

0 500 m
0 0.25 miles

Left Gagosian Gallery **Below** Whitney Museum of American Art

bringing a lively and contemporary feel to both the art and the environment.

One of the best things about this location is the indoor-outdoor experience offered by the number of different rooftops and terraces located on each floor. Starting from the top of the museum, you can view the streets of Manhattan from a sky-high distance, then gradually make your way downward, stopping on well-appointed roof terraces along the way. The museum is also home to Untitled, its highly rated on-site restaurant.

Friday evenings are a special treat, as the Whitney has 'Free Fridays.' From 7pm to 9:30pm, all patrons with or without a membership can browse the galleries for free. It draws an excellent crowd and remains the perfect way to spend an artful evening before dinner and a fun night out.

11 SING UP
at Marie's Crisis

MUSIC | CULTURE | NIGHTLIFE

Marie's Crisis is a favorite bar in the West Village because it offers an experience unlike any other: charming group sing-alongs to international hits, all of your pop favorites from numerous genres and eras, and classic Broadway tunes bring a sense of joy and New York camaraderie not to be missed.

ELIZABETH HOLMES/ALAMY STOCK PHOTO ©

📖 How To

Getting here 1 to Christopher St station.

When to go This bar is best on weekend evenings when the crowd is cheering and singing full-throttle.

Plan your songs Most of the sing-alongs are to old favorites everyone knows. But if you have a Broadway number you've always wanted to belt out at the top of your lungs, bring music!

MASSIMO SALESI/SHUTTERSTOCK ©

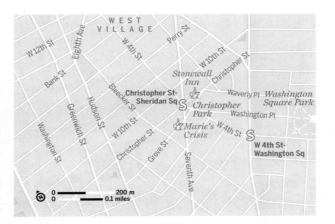

A Crisis of Fun

There really is no other experience in New York City quite like Marie's Crisis on Grove St in Greenwich Village. Broadway shows are the crowning glory of the city's theater scene and NYC-located iconic shows like *Rent, Avenue Q* and *West Side Story* have made the whole scene even more epic. But, unknown to many, there is more than one place to get your Broadway show-tune fix. If you've ever sat in your seat at a Broadway musical and wanted to get up to sing and dance along with the actors, then Marie's Crisis, just a quick subway ride away from Midtown, has everything you need.

The bar itself is quite historical, with roots going back to the 1850s when the space was a secret place for hosting prostitution. We don't know who Marie is, but her name and mysterious legacy live on every uproarious night at the Crisis, where singing is the new activity du jour. If you are a piano player, recreationally or professionally, this is the perfect avenue to show off your chops and be appreciated by an enormous round of applause after every number for keeping the party going. It's considered a dive bar, so the drinks are cheap and simple. An overly sweet rum-and-Coke out of a plastic cup has never tasted so good – we promise. Take a sip, raise your voice and sing your heart out among friends!

Top left Marie's Crisis
Bottom left Stonewall Inn

📖 History Lessons at Stonewall Inn

Stonewall Inn is a National Historic Landmark and a gay bar, and is widely known as the place where the civil rights movement for global LGBTIQ+ rights began. Late in the evening on June 28, 1969, police raided the bar, a discriminatory practice that was routine in the 1960s. Except, this time, the people resisted, demanding that they have the right to gather without fear of being arrested. A drink at this historic watering hole is a tribute to the sacrifices made by so many in the LGBTIQ+ community who demanded basic human rights.

12

Get Your Fashion
FIX AT FIT

FASHION | CULTURE | ART

Fashion and New York City have gone hand in hand since the dawn of time, and the city's fashion set continues to deliver with enthusiasm. Museum at Fashion Institute of Technology is an unforgettable experience of fashion past and present.

🗺️ How To

When to go Spring, summer and fall are best for walking the streets of north Chelsea. Museum at FIT is perfect for all seasons.

Getting here 1 to 28th St/Seventh Ave station, C/E to 23rd St/Eighth Ave station.

Getting around North Chelsea is best explored on foot or by bike.

Orientation FIT is just a short walk from the official Garment District of New York that begins on 34th St.

A Journey Through History with FIT Fashion

Over 100,000 people visit the Museum at Fashion Institute of Technology per year, and after even one walk through, you'll know why. One of the few specialized fashion museums in the world, the permanent collection houses 50,000 garments and accessories, including top designers Christian Dior, Coco Chanel and Balenciaga. The exhibition in the gallery is always showcasing 250 years of fashion, but the garments themselves rotate to keep the visuals fresh at all times. A favorite section is the Textile History Gallery, which tells a fascinating story about the history of looms, dyeing and weaving.

🚶 Gansevoort Street

Gansevoort St, a gorgeous cobblestoned street in the Meatpacking District part of West Village, is worth a stroll. It is home to some excellent high-end shopping and is only a short walk from the Whitney Museum of American Art and Chelsea Market.

Above left Fashion Institute of Technology **Above right** Gansevoort St **Left** Exhibition, Museum at FIT

Sustainability in Fashion

Fashion is one of the largest contributors to global carbon emissions. Fast fashion, the clothes made with and from large amounts of petroleum, are ubiquitous in the fashion industry. Polyester and other synthetic fabrics are petroleum heavy as a whole, which entwines the fashion industry with the same oil industry that contributes to pollution and climate change. An unsettling 1% of used clothing goes on to make a new garment, and New York City on its own puts 200 million pounds of clothing into landfills per year. A number of New York luxury fashion designers, such as Heron Preston, are working to turn this ship around. The Museum at FIT brings attention to the history of clothing's impact on the environment and allows consumers to reflect on their habits while also appreciating the beautiful garments on display.

🛍 Pippin Vintage Jewelry

Owned by two married GIA-certified Diamond Graders, Pippin Vintage Jewelry is one of the best vintage jewelry locations in the city. Upon entering the small shop, built from a hidden former carriage house on 17th St, you're swept away by the distinctive atmosphere. Old jazz greats like Ella Fitzgerald and Billie Holiday are playing, and you're surrounded by a beautiful 1920s scene arranged with glimmering necklaces, earrings, rings and other accessories. If you're looking for a singular vintage shopping experience surrounded by beauty, Pippin wins big.

28th St
Museum at
Fashion Institute
of Technology

W 28th St

28th St

W 27th St

CHELSEA

From Runway
With Love

FLATIRON
DISTRICT

Madison
Square
Park

Broadway

W 23rd St

23rd St

23rd St

Ninth Ave

Eighth Ave

Seventh Ave

Sixth Ave
(Avenue of the Americas)

Fifth Ave

W 19th St

W 18th St

INA

Pippin
Vintage
Jewelry

18th St

Gansevoort St
(0.25mi)

0 — 200 m
0 — 0.1 miles

Left Pippin Vintage Jewelry
Below Jeans in a thrift store

Thrift & Consignment Stores

A little-known fact about New York City is that it's filled with amazing thrift and consignment stores where you can buy some of the best secondhand clothes in the world. As sustainability in fashion becomes a more pressing issue, secondhand shopping is becoming more of a trend. The appreciation for the runway will never die, but as climate change becomes more and more real every moment, consignment is having its day in the sun. The best part is that New York offers luxury consignment, meaning you don't have to abstain from buying your favorite high-end labels. INA is the city's most established luxury consignment store along with From Runway with Love.

What You Can Do to Help

Changing the course of the fashion industry's dependence on petroleum, big oil companies and fossil fuels starts as much with the fashion industry as it does with the consumer. Even if you come to New York City to shop until you drop, also buy a few items from a consignment store. Consignment stores sell people's personal goods, like clothes or purses, through a third party vendor or thrift shop. Buying a few items secondhand from such a shop contributes to their growth and visibility, and to the sustainability of the fashion industry.

Fashion in New York City

A BRIEF HISTORY OF NYC STYLE

New York is a city that's forever evolving. From decade to decade, the city's creativity, economy and atmosphere bend with the times. Few other areas display this fascinating fluidity more than New York's fashion industry – read on to discover the untold science behind 'New York Style.'

Left Prada storefront, Fifth Avenue
Middle New York Fashion Week
Right Museum at FIT

VICTORIA LIPOV/SHUTTERSTOCK ©

The City of Personal Style

New York City fashion is a phenomenon that communicates the essence of the city. Everyone is entitled to be 100% themselves and own a unique personal style. The centrality of fashion to NYC may be curiously tied up with the impracticality of a personal car. In other cities automobiles often act as a manifestation of personal style. But in NYC, where walking is the most common method of transportation, your clothes are your 'car' and thus assume greater importance in communicating your personality!

The iconic image of Carrie Bradshaw, acted by Sarah Jessica Parker, gliding down Fifth Ave in her designer best is endlessly compelling for a reason – in New York City, style is everything! New York City is also a city of temperate climates, meaning there are four distinct seasons. Winter, spring, summer and autumn all come complete with their own unique styles and trends to suit the weather. Multiple television shows and films are filmed in New York City daily, so you could be an 'accidental' extra in the background of a major blockbuster or Emmy-winning show at any given moment – so, in some fashion, New Yorkers always seem to subconsciously 'dress the part.'

From the Garment District to NYFW

When you think of fashion in New York City, the mind goes to New York Fashion Week, glamorous runway shows and statuesque supermodels. However, it was the efforts of Manhattan's **Garment District**, located in a small 20 block radius from 34th St to 42nd St between Sixth and

Ninth Aves, that made it all possible. This area was once home to a multitude of factories that acted as one of the biggest garment-manufacturing hubs in the nation. At the end of WWI, the area held thousands of workers cutting fabrics, tailoring and making patterns that would influence the world of fashion for decades. In fact, global high-end labels like Donna Karan and Calvin Klein still operate out of the Garment District today.

With overseas production taking over the fashion industry, the Garment District faded from practical use, but the Fashion Institute of Technology (FIT; p76), located just below the district at 7th Ave and 27th St, keeps its history alive and flourishing. The Museum at the Fashion Institute of Technology is the Garment District's gem, and walking tours of the neighborhood are available to share its history and legacy.

From the iconic styles of Audrey Hepburn in *Breakfast at Tiffany's* and Meryl Streep in *The Devil Wears Prada* to a shoulder-padded Melanie Griffith in *Working Girl* and the unforgettable masculine-feminine style of Diane Keaton in *Annie Hall*, New York City fashion is indeed a phenomenon all its own. Cheers to the Garment District for starting it all!

> At the end of WWI, the Garment District held thousands of workers cutting fabrics, tailoring and making patterns that would influence the world of fashion for decades.

◎ The Met Costume Institute

The Met Costume Institute is another excellent resource for those looking for a dose of fashion history. The Costume Institute's collection is home to over 33,000 garments and objects covering seven centuries' worth of fashion for women, men and children. The Costume Institute was recently rebranded as the Anna Wintour Costume Center and gets funding from a generous endowment as well as various fundraisers throughout the year.

A trip to this fascinating museum, located on the Upper East Side, is an excellent complement to the Museum at the Fashion Institute of Technology.

TRINKETS
of Fashion History

01 The Old-Fashioned Garment District

New York City style was born in the unforgettable Garment District, once famous for its top tailors and seamstresses.

02 Donna Karan HQ

This living legend still has her flagship headquarters placed quite centrally in the Garment District – it's a must see!

03 Calvin Klein

Known for his clean and classic lines, this American designer forever calls New York City's garment district home.

04 Met Costume Institute

Heralded by the one and only Anna Wintour, Uptown's Met Costume Institute is a must-visit for fashion history.

05 Museum at FIT

This amazing locale is both a renowned university and expansive world-class fashion-history museum.

06 Pippin Vintage Jewelry

This Chelsea vintage shop (p78) is filled with sparkling rings, necklaces and more, and has a festive 1920s theme.

07 New York Fashion Week

The original fashion week started right in New York City, and every season the runways are yours to enjoy!

08 Madison Avenue

Madison Ave on the Upper East Side is known for its fabulous high-end boutiques.

Listings

BEST OF THE REST

☕ Strong Coffee & Sweet Treats

Jack's Coffee $

This small coffee shop off Greenwich Ave is a favorite for downtown locals and uptowners alike. Try the honey latte – it's delicious!

Magnolia Bakery $$

Although known for its excellent sweets, it's the banana pudding at this famous bakery that's the real winner. The hummingbird cupcakes come in at a close second place.

Billy's Bakery $

This Chelsea bakery is a neighborhood staple and has every sweet you could dream of in a bakery. Enjoy layer cakes, cupcakes, cookies, and party specials galore.

Ciao For Now $

Family-owned Ciao For Now offers delicious organic desserts and has an eclectic innovative menu. It also hosts private events and parties with catering.

Prodigy Coffee $

A minimal coffeehouse on Carmine St, Prodigy has a distinctly global feel and serves specialty coffee drinks with espressos from all over the world.

Fat Witch Bakery $

An absolutely adorable bakery, Fat Witch has some of the best brownies in New York. Located in Chelsea Market.

Molly's Cupcakes $

This special cupcake shop is known for its unique flavors like Boston Creme, Nutella, Ron Bennington and Blueberry Cheesecake. Make sure to try the filled cupcakes as well!

Doughnut Project $

Performing its craft with care, the Doughnut Project makes doughnuts in small batches with the finest ingredients, and New Yorkers come from far and wide to enjoy them.

🏞 Parks & Green Spaces

Washington Square Park

The best known of all of the West Village parks. New York University and the New School are nearby, giving it a consistently fun, youthful and energized vibe.

Union Square Park

Union Square is where the East Village and the West Village meet, so it's a major downtown nexus and meeting spot. Musicians and dancers make regular appearances.

Hudson River Park

Home to beautiful views, plenty of grassy areas to lie down in and a boardwalk for taking a jog or strolling with friends.

High Line

This breezy urban garden is located on a railway above the city streets. It's also an

Magnolia Bakery

inspiring sustainability project that is home to thousands of species of plants and flowers.

Chelsea Piers

A waterside playground, Chelsea Piers is an entertainment center catering to West Side Manhattan. Driving ranges, skating rink, wedding venues and great restaurants abound.

James J Walker Park

An excellent park on Hudson St, this is popular due to the many sports fields available for a wide assortment of athletic activities. Field hockey, soccer, basketball and many other sports are represented.

Bleecker Playground

This popular park is mostly frequented by families and parents, but if you're looking for a celebrity mom sighting in the West Village, this one's for you!

🥂 Specialty Cocktails & Dining

Morandi $$$

This Italian beauty is great for dining alfresco and has an amazing location on one of the most bustling streets in the neighborhood. The wine list is stellar.

Little Owl $$$

A tiny restaurant with limited seating, Little Owl has a delicious menu that's worth the wait. It's inspired by Mediterranean flavors but dishes run the gamut.

St Tropez West Village $$$

This gorgeous restaurant has phenomenal wine, a seafood-leaning menu and a nice assortment of oysters. The decor is warm and inviting, and it has a lively open kitchen.

While We Were Young Kitchen and Cocktails $$

This special space is part cocktail bar, part restaurant. It's stylish and airy, and the menu is primarily New American fare with a few twists.

Union Square Park

Little Branch $$

Little Branch is a small bar that serves specialty cocktails with unique flavors and profiles. The tequila and gin drinks are especially tasty and worth a try.

Employees Only $$

A speakeasy located in the heart of the neighborhood, this favorite never goes out of style. It has been voted 'World's Best Cocktail Bar' by the Spirited Awards.

City Winery $$$

This riverside winery not only has an excellent wine list and food menu, but also has live music events and other fun ticket parties to try!

The Spaniard $$

It's a mystery why this bar is called the Spaniard, as there is no Spanish decor or theme on the menus, but the big comfortable booths and stiff drinks are fantastic.

Analogue $$$

Located near both Washington Square Park and New York University, Analogue is known for its ultra-sophisticated setting and heavy-on-the-booze drinks. Cheers to that!

Scan to find more things to do in Chelsea & Greenwich Village online

BEN BRYANT/SHUTTERSTOCK ©

TRIBECA & THE FINANCIAL DISTRICT

CULTURE | ENTERTAINMENT | LEGACY

Experience Tribeca & the Financial District online

TRIBECA & THE FINANCIAL DISTRICT
Trip Builder

TAKE YOUR PICK OF MUST-SEES AND HIDDEN GEMS

No trip to Lower Manhattan would be complete without stops in Tribeca (Triangle Below Canal St) or the Financial District (FiDi for short). There's a bit of everything here: reminders of the city's history, renowned restaurants and plenty of sights. Because the avenues shorten as you move downtown, these neighborhoods feel more walkable, and it's easier to stroll from one side of the island to the other.

🗺 Neighborhood Notes

Best for City history, sightseeing and high-end dining.

Transport Any subway line except the orange BDFM or light green G.

Getting around Traffic and construction, combined with one-way and cobblestone streets, suit walking best.

Tip Hang out on the steps by the New York Stock Exchange for prime people-watching.

TRIBECA

Challenge your friends to mini-golf, then cool off with a drink by the water at **Pier 25** (p91).
🚶 *8 min from Franklin St station*

Greenwich St

W Broadway

Vesey St

Take the elevator to **One World Observatory** (p97) at the top of One World Trade Center and catch the view from the tallest building in the United States.
🚶 *2 min from World Trade Center station*

West St (West Side Hwy)

BATTERY PARK CITY

Hudson River

Dig into your wallet for a day full of shopping at high-end stores in **Brookfield Place** (p97)
🚶 *8 min from World Trade Center station*

Robert F Wagner Jr Park

Upper New York Bay

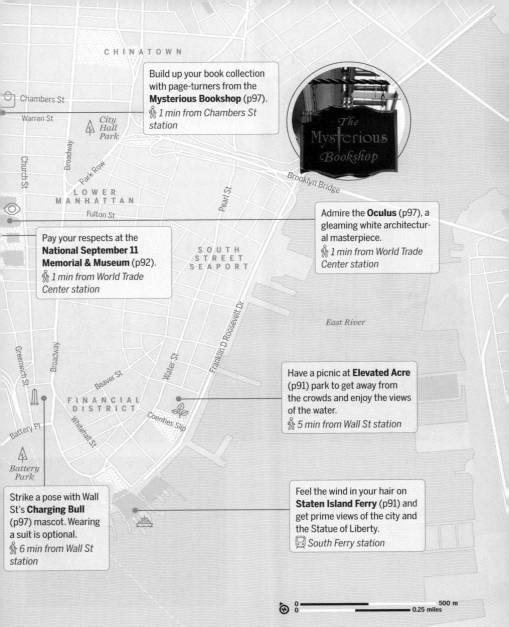

CHINATOWN

Chambers St

Warren St

City Hall Park

Broadway

Park Row

Pearl St

LOWER MANHATTAN

Fulton St

Church St

Brooklyn Bridge

Build up your book collection with page-turners from the **Mysterious Bookshop** (p97).
🚶 1 min from Chambers St station

Admire the **Oculus** (p97), a gleaming white architectural masterpiece.
🚶 1 min from World Trade Center station

Pay your respects at the **National September 11 Memorial & Museum** (p92).
🚶 1 min from World Trade Center station

SOUTH STREET SEAPORT

Franklin D Roosevelt Dr

East River

Greenwich St

Broadway

Beaver St

Water St

FINANCIAL DISTRICT

Whitehall St

Coenties Slip

Battery Pl

Battery Park

Have a picnic at **Elevated Acre** (p91) park to get away from the crowds and enjoy the views of the water.
🚶 5 min from Wall St station

Strike a pose with Wall St's **Charging Bull** (p97) mascot. Wearing a suit is optional.
🚶 6 min from Wall St station

Feel the wind in your hair on **Staten Island Ferry** (p91) and get prime views of the city and the Statue of Liberty.
🚆 South Ferry station

0
0
500 m
0.25 miles

13

A Day by the
WATER

SCENIC | RECREATION | ARCHITECTURE

Put on your most comfortable walking shoes and stroll down and across the tip of Manhattan, where piers jut into the Hudson and East Rivers on all sides of the island. Catch a breeze off the waves and take in spectacular views of Brooklyn and New Jersey.

JAMES ANDREWS/SJ/SHUTTERSTOCK ©

🗺 How To

Getting here Take the subway to downtown Manhattan below Canal St, then walk west or east until you hit the water.

When to go Skip winter, when below-freezing temperatures merge with a bone-chilling wind off the water.

Tip Bring your camera and take in a sunset across the waves.

PHILIP LANGE/SHUTTERSTOCK ©

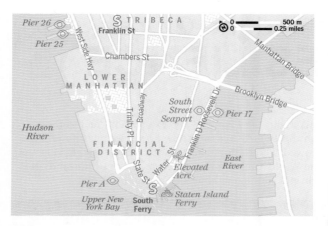

Top left Pier 25, Hudson River Park
Bottom left Pier 17

Turn up the competition Challenge your peers to a game of mini-golf or grab a kayak and race them to the water at **Hudson River Park** (hudsonriverpark.org), which includes **Piers 25 and 26** in Tribeca. There's also a skate park, bike lanes, a dog park and plenty of greenery to soak up the sun.

Awe-inducing architecture Pier A in the Financial District is one of New York City's most historic piers, home to a harbor house that was built in 1886 and restored into a bar and restaurant complex in 2014. The architecture and clock tower are worth a look, and if you step up to the waterfront, you'll get a clear view of the **Statue of Liberty**.

Bring on the boats All aboard! If you want to see sails so high they appear to touch the sky, head to **South Street Seaport** (theseaport.nyc) in the Financial District. When you're done admiring the ships, grab food at one of the countless restaurants. If you're lucky, a street fair may be going on in the cobblestone square, or you can browse one-of-a-kind boutiques in the area. If you're really feeling adventurous, head down to South Ferry to take the **Staten Island Ferry** past the Statue of Liberty and into a whole new borough.

Live music and city lights Don't miss a nighttime concert on the roof of **Pier 17** (pier17ny.com). Your ticket gets you a memorable performance in front of a sweeping view of the Brooklyn Bridge.

☼ Escape the Noise

You don't need to trek uptown for greenery and some solitude. Not far from the Battery, which can get busy when the weather's pleasant, there's the little-known **Elevated Acre** park atop a garage in the Financial District overlooking the water. It may not be a pier, but it's within walking distance of the piers on the East Side, and its higher altitude means the views stretch a little further. If you like watching helicopters take off and land, you may see a couple from this perch. The best part, however, is how few people seem to know about this hidden escape, so don't be surprised if you're lucky enough to get the place to yourself.

Behind the City's
RESILIENCE

HISTORY | LEGACY | PRIDE

It's impossible to talk about the Financial District without mentioning the 2001 terrorist attack on the Twin Towers and how Lower Manhattan rebuilt itself in the years that followed. The National September 11 Memorial & Museum (911memorial.org) and One World Trade Center (wtc.com) attract thousands of visitors, and pride shines bright in the neighborhood's local businesses.

RESUL MUSLU/SHUTTERSTOCK ©

How To

Getting here Take the blue A/C/E lines straight to World Trade Center station.

When to go If visiting in winter or summer, dress for the chill and the humidity respectively.

Fact Bowling Green park is NYC's oldest park and is said to have once been a council ground for Native American tribes.

LITTLENYSTOCK/SHUTTERSTOCK ©

Support small businesses After 9/11, there was a sharp decline in mom-and-pop shops in Lower Manhattan, but now the neighborhood is busy and bustling. From jewelers to independent booksellers to coffee shops to wine stores, there's something for everyone. With its walkable streets and historic alleyways, the area feels more quaint and manageable than, say, the Midtown office districts.

Follow the cobblestone road There are plenty of folks in suits around here, but they bring hefty business to the local restaurants and bars who need it most. Grab a bite or a beer at any establishment on **Stone St**'s narrow cobblestone path to blend in with the hordes of people looking to unwind after work. The outdoor picnic tables make it easy to strike up a conversation with someone new or bring a big group of friends.

Rebirth after rebirth The history etched in the Financial District's streets stretches back 400 hundred years, and the area has weathered not just a historic terrorist attack, but also hurricanes, pandemics and more disasters. Time and time again, it always rebounds stronger than ever. For example, **Trinity Church** near the New York Stock Exchange was the first church in the city and has been rebuilt thrice. It was burned down during the American Revolution, then devastated by a snowstorm in the 1800s.

Top left National September 11 Memorial **Bottom left** Stone St

🍸 A Taste of History

Fancy a drink at the same pub George Washington once visited? **Fraunces Tavern** (frauncestavern. com) on Pearl St in the Financial District is widely known as New York's oldest bar and has a long history that lives on in its very own museum. It's survived, among other things, wars, storms and pandemics over the past 250 years, but it's still standing and is an ideal place to grab a bite to eat and a nice pint or whiskey. Depending on the season, enjoy happy-hour oysters there, plus live music on weekends.

NYC Behind the
SCENES

CINEMA | ENTERTAINMENT | FESTIVAL

▬▬▬ Entertainment fans, this is the neighborhood for you. Countless movies and television shows have been shot in Lower Manhattan, and this is a prime area to take a walking tour of filming locations or check out a few fan favorites. Don't forget to treat yourself to a movie at an intimate theater like Roxy Cinema (roxyhotelnyc.com), featuring gourmet popcorn and craft cocktails.

OLDSKOOLDESIGN/SHUTTERSTOCK ©

🗺 How To

Getting here 1 to Franklin St station, A/C/E to Canal St station.

When to go Anytime is a good time, but the annual Tribeca Festival, typically held in April, attracts sto-rytellers and independent filmmakers from around the globe.

Tip Keep your eyes peeled for celebrity sightings, as many famous music artists, actors and actresses live in the area.

DW LABS INCORPORATED/SHUTTERSTOCK ©

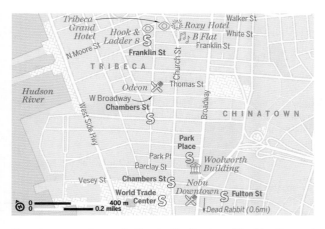

Tribeca Grand Hotel
Hook & Ladder 8
Roxy Hotel
B Flat
Walker St
White St
Franklin St
N Moore St
Franklin St
TRIBECA
Church St
Thomas St
Hudson River
Odeon
W Broadway
Chambers St
Broadway
CHINATOWN
West Side Hwy
Park Place
Park Pl
Barclay St
Woolworth Building
Vesey St
Chambers St
Nobu Downtown
World Trade Center
Fulton St
400 m
0.2 miles
Dead Rabbit (0.6mi)

Experience movie magic Stop by the **Hook and Ladder 8 firehouse**, which you'll recognize as the original *Ghostbusters* headquarters, then swing by the **Tribeca Grand Hotel** where Hugh Grant filmed *Two Weeks Notice*. Then head to the famed **Woolworth Building** on Broadway, where Nicholas Cage went hunting for *National Treasure* and where Amy Adams faces off against her character's evil stepmother in *Enchanted*. Top it all off with brunch at the **Odeon**, known for creating *Sex and the City*'s beloved cosmopolitan cocktail.

Celebrity business ventures You never know who you may catch dining at one of the area's celebrity-owned establishments. Robert De Niro is involved with several restaurants nearby: grab sushi at his **Nobu Downtown**, fill up on pasta at his **Locanda Verde**, or enjoy a fine glass of wine at his **Tribeca Grill**. In the morning, get your caffeine fix at Hugh Jackman's **Laughing Man Coffee**, which prioritizes sustainability and donates proceeds to charity.

Stories that stick with you The **Tribeca Film Festival**, also made famous by De Niro, was born in the aftermath of the September 11th attacks to help revive downtown Manhattan. It's now one of the few festivals that celebrates immersive experiences, audio storytelling and video games in addition to independent film. If you're in town for it, you're guaranteed to find something that piques your interest in its lineup.

Top left Hook and Ladder 8 firehouse
Bottom left Roxy Hotel

♪♪ Feel the Music

Top off your day of Hollywood magic with a little jazz and blues at one of the handful of live-music bars in Tribeca. The **Django**, in the basement of the Roxy Hotel, is a popular choice and can get packed on weekends. If it's full, try the B Flat lounge on Church St or head downtown to FiDi's **Dead Rabbit** on Water St to sample its famous Irish whiskey during a traditional Irish live-music session. Another option: stay at the Roxy and catch a cinematic classic at its intimate movie theater just steps away from its jazz club.

Listings

BEST OF THE REST

✖️ Sit-Down Dining

Odeon $$$

The best place for a cosmo alongside a high-end brunch or bistro favorites. Always packed with families and friends catching up over a few drinks. Reliably good food.

Manhatta $$$

Get a bird's-eye view of the city from this 60th-floor restaurant featuring a chef-curated seasonal menu and Burgundy wines.

Crown Shy $$$

You can't go wrong with the New American eats here. It also has a seasonal menu, so you never have to get the same thing twice.

CUT by Wolfgang Puck $$$

In the Four Seasons Hotel New York Downtown; splurge on a steak and exquisite cocktail here.

Eataly $$$

Grab Italian groceries here or sit down for pasta you won't forget. Unlike its Uptown location, the Downtown Eataly market doesn't sell wine.

Tamarind Tribeca $$$

High-end Indian food worth writing home about. Try everything from chicken to lamb to goat to seafood here.

City Vineyard $$

Fuel up at this popular spot for boozy brunch that overlooks the water. With its world-class wine menu, it's also a great spot for an outdoor post-work happy hour.

Benvenuto Tribeca $

Good 24-hour dining is hard to come by in Tribeca and FiDi, but this diner serves it all, all the time. It delivers to your door, too!

🍺 Nightlife

Stone Street Tavern $$

The hub of FiDi's famed Stone St; stop by for a pint or two.

Watermark $$

For a drink outside by the water, this is your spot.

IPIC $$

Settle in for a movie at this luxury theater, which is perfect for wining and dining.

Clinton Hall $$

If beer halls are your thing and the weather has forced Stone St's picnic tables indoors, this is your best bet.

📷 Architecture Worth the Picture

Woolworth Building

Get a glimpse of what skyscrapers used to look like. From 1913 to 1930, this was the tallest building in the world.

Staple Street Skybridge

Three stories off the ground, this bridge connects two separate buildings over one of Tribeca's shortest streets. It's one of the neighborhood's most popular photo destinations.

'Jenga' Building at 56 Leonard St

This one's easy to find. Look up and search for a skyscraper with apartments teetering over one another like a Jenga game. It's a residential building that just looks really, really cool.

St Paul's Chapel

This historic chapel dates back to the 1700s and welcomes visitors throughout the year.

Trinity Church

Dating back to 1697, Trinity Church has a Gothic Revival style. Founding Father Alexander Hamilton is buried here.

Oculus

The bright white wings of the Oculus are impossible to miss while walking around Ground Zero. In fact, Spanish architect Santiago Calatrava designed it to look like a bird.

One World Observatory

Perched at the top of One World Trade Center (Freedom Tower), aka the tallest building in the Western Hemisphere, One World Observatory offers unparalleled views of the city.

☼ Outdoor Sights

National September 11 Memorial & Museum

The site of the Twin Towers. Remember and pay your respects to victims of the 2001 terrorist attack that shaped NYC history.

Fearless Girl

This bronze sculpture by Kristen Visbal has made its way around FiDi as a symbol of resilience. It was originally placed in front of the *Charging Bull* statue, but in 2018 she found a new home facing the New York Stock Exchange. A plaque of her footprints remains next to the bull as a reminder of her time there.

Charging Bull

Sculptor Arturo Di Modica built this famed bull out of bronze and surprised the whole neighborhood by placing it outside the New York Stock Exchange in 1989, two years after a big stock-market crash. It's since become a symbol of Wall St and today sits next to Bowling Green park.

SPIROVIEW INC/SHUTTERSTOCK ©

Battery

Battery

Get your nature fix at this low-key park. It's less crowded than Madison Square Park or Central Park further uptown.

SeaGlass Carousel

At the Battery, there's a magnificent carousel both kids and adults will appreciate. It's less of a fun carnival ride and more of an immersive artistic experience.

🛍 Shopping

Mysterious Bookshop

Addicted to true crime? Get your fill of whodunit stories and tall tales of espionage and murder here. The store was opened in 1979 and specializes in rare books and first editions.

Brookfield Place

Malls are rare in New York City, but this massive shopping center is great for both window-shopping and grabbing lunch. Hudson Eats, inside Brookfield Place, is a gourmet food court featuring every cuisine imaginable.

Scan to find more things to do in Tribeca & the Financial District online

TRIBECA & THE FINANCIAL DISTRICT REVIEWS

SOHO & CHINATOWN

HISTORY | FOOD | SHOPS

Experience
SoHo &
Chinatown
online

SOHO & CHINATOWN
Trip Builder

TAKE YOUR PICK OF MUST-SEES AND HIDDEN GEMS

▬▬ SoHo (South of Houston) and Chinatown are home to all the things that make New York City special. Houston St down to Canal St is a shopper's paradise, with big-name stores, pop-ups and trendy boutiques. NYC's Chinatown, meanwhile, is the largest in the country and is bustling with markets and a rich history of blended cultures.

🗺 Neighborhood Notes

Best for Window-shopping, snacking, exploring speakeasies, photos worthy of social media and street fashion.

Transport For SoHo N/Q/R line to Prince St. For Chinatown N/Q/R to Canal St.

Getting around Walking is the best way to see the neighborhood.

Tip Most shoppers crowd around Broadway, so walk along Mercer or Greene Sts for less foot traffic.

Find the famous cronut, a croissant-doughnut mash-up, at **Dominique Ansel Bakery** (p113).
🚶 7 min from Spring St station

Spring St
Spring St
Thompson St
W Broadway

Hunt for vintage designer finds at **What Goes Around Comes Around** (p103), where you'll find luxury items at attainable prices.
🚶 5 min from Spring St station

Canal St

Shop from local vendors and grab a bite at the selection of pop-up restaurants at **Canal St Market** (p107).
🚶 2 min from Canal St station

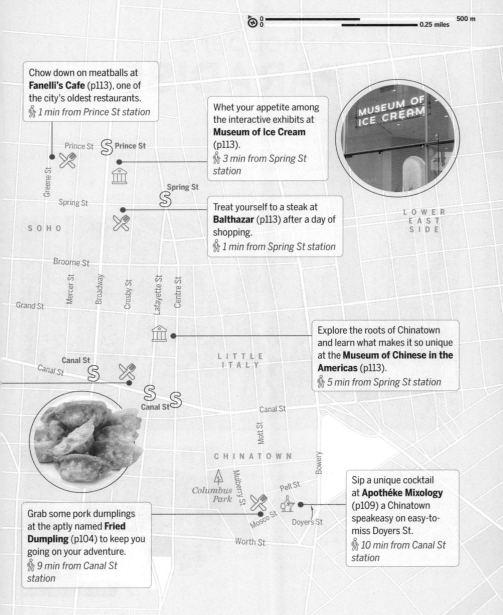

Chow down on meatballs at **Fanelli's Cafe** (p113), one of the city's oldest restaurants.
🚶 *1 min from Prince St station*

Whet your appetite among the interactive exhibits at **Museum of Ice Cream** (p113).
🚶 *3 min from Spring St station*

Treat yourself to a steak at **Balthazar** (p113) after a day of shopping.
🚶 *1 min from Spring St station*

Explore the roots of Chinatown and learn what makes it so unique at the **Museum of Chinese in the Americas** (p113).
🚶 *5 min from Spring St station*

Sip a unique cocktail at **Apothéke Mixology** (p109) a Chinatown speakeasy on easy-to-miss Doyers St.
🚶 *10 min from Canal St station*

Grab some pork dumplings at the aptly named **Fried Dumpling** (p104) to keep you going on your adventure.
🚶 *9 min from Canal St station*

Prince St

Prince St

Spring St

Spring St

Greene St

Mercer St

Broadway

Crosby St

Lafayette St

Centre St

Grand St

Broome St

Spring St

Canal St

Canal St

Canal St

Canal St

Mott St

Bowery

Mulberry St

Pell St

Doyers St

Mosco St

Worth St

Columbus Park

SOHO

LITTLE ITALY

CHINATOWN

LOWER EAST SIDE

0   500 m
0   0.25 miles

16 A Shopper's
PARADISE

TRENDS | FASHION | PEOPLE-WATCHING

SoHo is renowned for its shopping, with streets full of luxury boutiques, high-end designs and flagship stores for some of the biggest brands in the country. If you're looking to window-shop, pick up gifts for loved ones, or reinvent your personal style, this is a must-see neighborhood. SoHo is most famous for its runway labels, but savvy shoppers can find stores to suit any budget.

RYAN DEBERARDINIS/SHUTTERSTOCK ©

🗺 How To

Getting here N/Q/R lines to Prince St station, the heart of SoHo's most popular shopping area.

When to go Spring and fall are best, sidestepping the humidity of summer and the holiday-shopping rush of winter.

Sidestreet shuffle
Explore the side streets: Mercer, Spring, Wooster and more. There's less foot traffic and just as many enticing sights.

Refuel Visit much-loved **Prince Street Pizza** to taste its signature crispy, curled pepperoni.

RESUL MUSLU/SHUTTERSTOCK ©

Wardrobe refresh Switch up your style by visiting any one of the countless boutiques or household-name stores in SoHo. Nearly every US retailer you can imagine has a location here, so it's easy to spend a whole day flipping through clothing racks and trying stuff on to find your next favorite outfit. If you prefer to shop sustainably, **Housing Works** on Crosby St and **What Goes Around Comes Around** on Wooster St are your best bets for vintage finds.

Get inspired You don't need to pull out your wallet to appreciate SoHo. This is hands-down one of the best areas of Manhattan for street fashion. You can spot all the latest fashion trends in SoHo, whether they're on people walking by or in the store windows. It's worth walking around just to see how stylish everyone looks, and how the very concept of style varies from person to person. When you walk (or strut) with confidence, any outfit becomes high fashion!

Catch the unexpected Because SoHo is such a hot destination for shoppers, it's a prime location for limited-time pop-ups and immersive experiences. Several buildings operate as event spaces that rotate through different events, so you never know what new cool thing you may see. Sometimes it's an artist exhibition, a social-media-friendly museum, a highly anticipated sample sale with a line out the door, or something else! Don't be afraid to pop into random stores just to see what's going on.

Top left Spring St and Broadway intersection **Bottom left** Ladurée

☕ Pick-Me-Ups

If you're a fan of tea, get your caffeine fix at **Harney & Sons Fine Teas' SoHo Shop** (harney. com) on Broome St. The third-generation family business has an extensive collection of teas you can sample in its in-house cafe, and the staff can answer any questions you may have about brewing, ingredients or flavors. If you need something a little stronger, try the coffee and sweet treats at French bakery (and celebrity favorite) **Maman** (mamannyc.com) on Centre St, or get brunch and delectable macarons at **Ladurée** (laduree.us) on West Broadway.

TASTE THE FLAVORS
of Chinatown

01 Dr Clark's

Come with a group and share the foods of Japanese island Hokkaido. Sea urchin and mutton are must-haves.

02 Fried Dumpling

For under $2, you get five pork pot stickers, arguably one of the city's most delicious steals.

03 Peking Duck House

If you're in the mood for duck, this is the place. Don't forget to BYOB (bring your own booze).

04 Original Chinatown Ice Cream Factory

This isn't your standard ice-cream shop. Taste test a wide variety of flavors, from black sesame to lychee to red bean.

05 Mei Li Wah

Order the char siu bao, a pork bun that'll satisfy your sweet tooth.

06 Tasty Hand-Pulled Noodles

Get your pan-fried noodle fix here. There's a reason the lines get so long.

07 Golden Diner
Chef Sam Yoo is an expert at putting an Asian spin on diner favorites like burgers and pancakes.

08 Hop Kee
Come here for Cantonese-style snails and crabs.

09 Jing Fong Restaurant
There's no shortage of dim sum spots in Chinatown, but this is a favorite. With over 500 seats, you're practically guaranteed a table.

10 Pinklady Cheese Tart
Get fluffy Japanese-baked cheese tarts in flavors like matcha, ube and chocolate.

11 Pho Vietnam
Bring your appetite for pork banh mi or a hearty bowl of pho.

12 Buddha Bodai
Diners will find a dim sum menu with 100% vegetarian options.

13 Kam Hing Coffee Shop
Sip on tea and get the sponge cake for a perfect afternoon pick-me-up.

17 CRUISE
Down Canal Street

CULTURE | COMMUNITY | ART

■■■■■ Canal St is one of those rare streets that stretches across almost all of Manhattan from west to east, with various neighborhoods to its north and south. That makes it a prime street to stroll down and witness how quickly the city's vibes change from block to block. To the south of Canal is Tribeca, then Chinatown; to the north are SoHo and Little Italy, among other areas.

RICHARD LEVINE/ALAMY STOCK PHOTO ©

🗺 Trip Notes

Getting here Take the 1, A/C/E, or N/Q/R/W lines to Canal St station. The 1 will take you to the westmost point of the street, so get off there to walk from Tribeca's borders across to Chinatown.

When to go Anytime you like, as long as you're dressed for the weather.

Tip Keep your eyes peeled for pop-up art galleries as you walk down Canal St. Depending on the season, artists take over storefronts and transform them into exhibitions that are visual and sometimes interactive.

🚶 Canal Street

Canal St was named after an 1800s-era canal that no longer exists. Now various shops, cafes and art galleries line the sidewalks, and it's not uncommon to see bumper-to-bumper traffic along the way. That's why walking is the most efficient way to soak up the sights and watch the city change and evolve with every step.

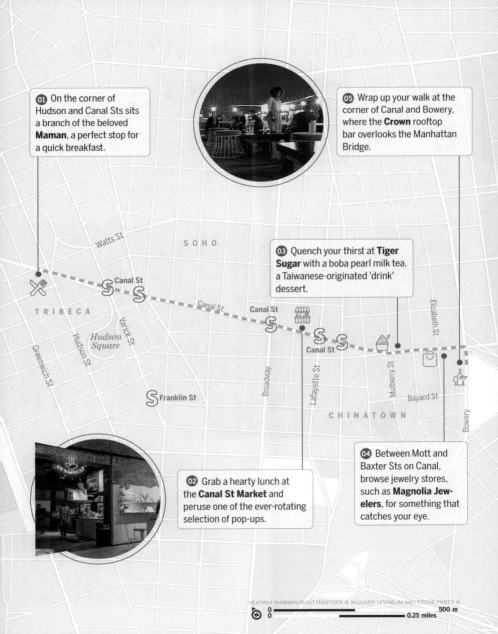

01 On the corner of Hudson and Canal Sts sits a branch of the beloved **Maman**, a perfect stop for a quick breakfast.

05 Wrap up your walk at the corner of Canal and Bowery, where the **Crown** rooftop bar overlooks the Manhattan Bridge.

03 Quench your thirst at **Tiger Sugar** with a boba pearl milk tea, a Taiwanese-originated 'drink' dessert.

02 Grab a hearty lunch at the **Canal St Market** and peruse one of the ever-rotating selection of pop-ups.

04 Between Mott and Baxter Sts on Canal, browse jewelry stores, such as **Magnolia Jewelers**, for something that catches your eye.

Watts St

SOHO

Canal St

Canal St

Canal St

Canal St

Canal St

Elizabeth St

TRIBECA

Varick St

Hudson St

Hudson Square

Greenwich St

Broadway

Lafayette St

Mulberry St

Bayard St

Bowery

Franklin St

CHINATOWN

0   500 m
0   0.25 miles

18 Doyers Street's Dark
HISTORY

HISTORY | NIGHTLIFE | ART

▬▬▬ Doyers St, sandwiched between Bowery and Pell Sts, and one of Chinatown's most legendary blocks, holds hundreds of years' worth of stories in its bones, despite being a mere 200ft long. It's a quick walk, but you'll want to explore what's become of the street's bloody history. Today, it's a secluded nightlife destination.

RBLIMP/SHUTTERSTOCK ©

🗺 How To

Getting here Take the 6 to Canal St station or the 4/5/6 to Brooklyn Bridge-City Hall station. It's a 10-minute walk from there, or take a bus to E Broadway/Catherine St or Bowery/Bayard St for a shorter walk.

When to go Anytime!

Tip In 2021, to revive the neighborhood following the economic effects of the Covid-19 pandemic, Doyers St was taken over by a 4800-sq-ft asphalt art mural called *Rice Terraces*.

LITTLENYSTOCK/SHUTTERSTOCK ©

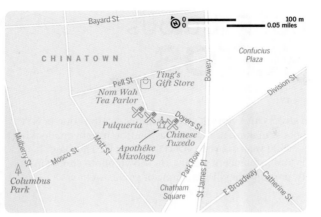

The map shows:
- Bayard St
- CHINATOWN
- Confucius Plaza
- Pell St
- Ting's Gift Store
- Bowery
- Nom Wah Tea Parlor
- Division St
- Pulqueria
- Doyers St
- Chinese Tuxedo
- Mulberry St
- Mosco St
- Mott St
- Apothéke Mixology
- Park Row
- Columbus Park
- Chatham Square
- St James Pl
- E Broadway
- Catherine St
- 100 m / 0.05 miles

Top left Doyers St **Bottom left** Nom Wah Tea Parlor

Feel the chemistry Taste the delectable cocktail concoctions at **Apothéke Mixology** (apothekemixology.com), a first-come-first-served speakeasy hidden away on Doyers St. It hosts classes where you can learn firsthand what liqueurs and herbs do (and don't!) go together. And to really mix things up, hop over to the neighboring **Pulqueria** (pulquerianyc.com), a former Vietnamese sandwich shop turned Mexican restaurant and bar.

Doyers Street dim sum Nom Wah Tea Parlor (nomwah.com) has been serving up delicious dim sum and dumplings since 1920, but got its start as a beloved neighborhood bakery. You can't go wrong with any of its desserts, like the $2 almond cookie or steamed red-bean buns for $4.50.

Tchotchkes galore Ting's Gift Store on the corner of Doyers has a plethora of trinkets that will catch your eye. Do you need any porcelain figurines, wind chimes or incense? Probably not. Will you buy it anyway for the dopamine rush of an impulse purchase? Most certainly.

Heart of history Get dinner at **Chinese Tuxedo** (chinesetuxedo.com), where you'll enjoy modern dishes in a building with decades of history in its bones. This was once NYC's first Chinese theater, aka the Chinese Opera House, where gang wars reportedly erupted in the early 1900s. Doyers St was eventually dubbed 'The Bloody Angle' or 'Murder Alley' because of this dark history.

The Bloody Angle

Doyers St became a prime spot for murder in part because of how crooked and secluded the street is. Its sharp bend — thus, 'The Bloody Angle' — made it difficult to see who was waiting for you around the corner. Journey into the depths of Doyers by exploring its tunnel, which helped people escape a bloody ending back in the day. Before the Chinese Tuxedo restaurant came to be, you could enter the tunnel from Doyers St itself, but now your best bet is to enter through what used to be the exit in Chatham Sq's Wing Fat Mansion.

19 Shoot Fabulous
PHOTOS

FASHION | PHOTOGRAPHY | ART

████ With its cobblestone streets and vibrant street fashion, SoHo is one of NYC's most photogenic neighborhoods, making it a prime destination for anyone looking to squeeze in a few pictures while wearing your #OOTD (Outfit Of The Day). It's common to see both models and influencers staging their own photo shoots in the streets, and if you ask nicely, perhaps they'll snap a pic of you as well.

🍴 Snack Snaps

Remember to photograph the delicious eats you've enjoyed along the way. SoHo has great brunch spots, many with quaint outdoor seating that puts you in the center of the action. So include in your next pic the mimosa or iced coffee next to your gourmet avocado toast or eggs Benedict. Visit **Cha Cha Matcha** on Broome St if you need an Instagram-worthy drink.

🗺 Trip Notes

Getting here Blue C/E line to Spring St station, or yellow N/R line to Prince St station.

When to go Pleasant, slightly overcast weather makes for the best photos.

Fashion SoHo was once Manhattan's prime district for artists, and with all its fashion-forward boutiques creativity is still its strong suit.

Restrooms Bloomingdales on Broadway is one of the few area stores with restrooms open to the public.

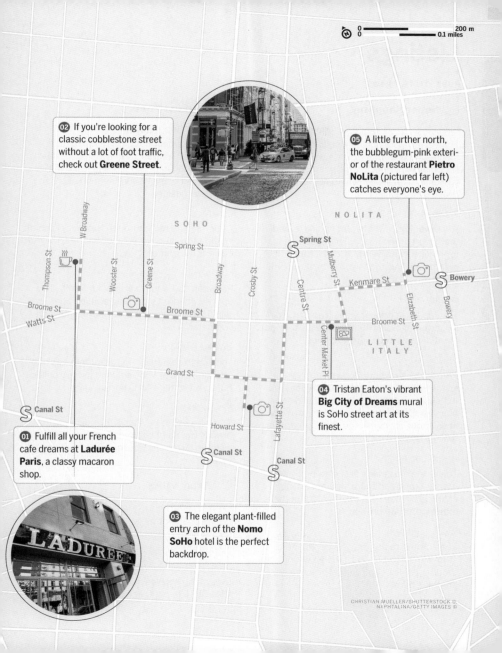

02 If you're looking for a classic cobblestone street without a lot of foot traffic, check out **Greene Street**.

05 A little further north, the bubblegum-pink exterior of the restaurant **Pietro NoLita** (pictured far left) catches everyone's eye.

NOLITA

SOHO

Spring St

Spring St

W Broadway

Thompson St

Wooster St

Greene St

Broadway

Crosby St

Centre St

Mulberry St

Kenmare St

Bowery

Elizabeth St

Bowery

Broome St

Broome St

Watts St

Broome St

Center Market Pl

LITTLE ITALY

Grand St

Canal St

Howard St

Lafayette St

04 Tristan Eaton's vibrant **Big City of Dreams** mural is SoHo street art at its finest.

01 Fulfill all your French cafe dreams at **Ladurée Paris**, a classy macaron shop.

Canal St

Canal St

03 The elegant plant-filled entry arch of the **Nomo SoHo** hotel is the perfect backdrop.

Listings

BEST OF THE REST

🛍 Super Shopping

Nike Store

There's always a unique installation on the ground floor of this massive five-story shopping experience, which has included customization stations to make your purchase uniquely yours.

Artists & Fleas

You never know what you'll find here, and that's part of the magic. This space brings together various vendors, collectors and creators selling goods you didn't know you needed.

Uniqlo

The Japanese retailer stays true to its roots at its sprawling SoHo location. This is the spot for affordable, high-quality basics.

REI

Prepare for the outdoors with everything inside REI's flagship store, which boasts a full-service bike shop, plus a ski and snowboard shop. Whatever questions you may have about your gear, the staff are experts ready to help.

Alexander Wang

This is the designer's first-ever brick-and-mortar store, and there's always an interesting art installation to check out at the entrance as you browse.

Bloomingdales

There aren't many get-it-all department stores in SoHo, but you can't go wrong with Bloomingdales. You can find practically anything here.

💝 Boutique Finds

Wolf & Badger

Support independent designers creating products for women, men and your home. The SoHo location is the brand's first in the US and showcases a combination of US and European designs.

Creatures of Comfort

After rising to fame through New York Fashion Week, Jade Lai creates functional and playful designs for women.

Makié

For when you want to treat your family. This upscale children's clothing boutique has minimalist designs fit for a budding fashion superstar.

Broken English

Looking to splurge or just admire things that sparkle? Peruse one-of-a-kind jewelry collections and vintage finds here.

Kirna Zabete

This concept store stacks its racks with brands like Saint Laurent, Valentino and more, all expertly curated for the fashionista inside you.

🖼 Artsy Vibes

Drawing Center

Get inspired at this nonprofit organization showcasing drawing exhibitions both modern and historic.

Leslie-Lohman Museum of Art

Everything you see at this museum presents the LGBTIQ+ perspective, whether it's art from the queer community or a piece inspired by it.

Angelika Film Center

Catch independent cinema, along with blockbuster favorites, almost every night. Its cafe also serves beer and wine.

Trendy Bars

Gitano $$$

Feel like you're in Tulum at this seasonal open-air restaurant and bar off Canal St. The cocktails are pricey, but you're paying for the ambience. It's known for its mezcal.

Crosby Bar $$$

This lounge in the Crosby Hotel is bright and cheerful, with food and drinks to satisfy even the pickiest people.

Botanica $

If dive bars are more your scene, try this Houston St favorite where, if you're lucky, there may be some impromptu karaoke.

Tyger $$$

Come for the cocktails, but don't sleep on the delicious starters. Get the house-made egg noodles and wash it down with any drink that has lychee in it.

✖ Food

Fanelli's Cafe $$

Since 1847, Fanelli's has served up classic diner food you can't go wrong with.

Dominique Ansel Bakery $

Don't be surprised if there's a line of cronut fans outside. Cronuts are like if croissants and doughnuts had a baby, and they're a specialty here. Pro tip: order delivery if you want the deliciousness without the wait.

Balthazar $$$

Get your French cuisine, and don't forget about their raw bar featuring oysters, clams, and various shellfish.

Fried Dumpling $

Real-deal, no-frills fried dumplings.

Antique Garage $$$

For a unique ambience and a blend of Turkish, Greek and Italian flavours, try brunch or dinner here.

Van Leeuwen Ice Cream $

Beat the heat with one of the city's most famous ice-cream shops. You'll find both traditional and unique flavours, and there are vegan options, too.

La Mercerie $$$

This French cafe is the perfect spot to sip a coffee, nibble on a fresh pastry, and have a deep conversation or read a book solo. You can have a hearty sit-down meal if you prefer, but it's easier on your wallet and you still get the vibe with a light afternoon snack.

🏛 Museums

Museum of Ice Cream

You can't miss this bright, cheerful building as you stroll down Broadway. This interactive museum will satisfy your sweet tooth and provide plenty of colorful photo opportunities along the way.

Museum of Chinese in the Americas

Dig deeper into Chinese American history with over 85,000 artifacts that teach you how and why Chinatown's culture, as well as Chinese American traditions more broadly, evolved into what it is today.

 Scan to find more things to do in SoHo & Chinatown online

BROOKLYN

HIP | INNOVATIVE | DIVERSE

Experience Brooklyn online

BROOKLYN
Trip Builder

TAKE YOUR PICK OF MUST-SEES AND HIDDEN GEMS

▬▬▬ Brooklyn might be synonymous with artsy-fartsy hipsterdom, but NYC's most populous borough is more than beards and bikes. It's Biggie Smalls and Barbra Streisand; industrial chic and immigrant grown. Grab a craft brew, hit up a warehouse party and saunter along the shoreline to uncover why Kings County is the global epicenter of 'cool.'

🗺 Neighborhood Notes

Best for Dynamic parks, trendy nightlife, picturesque neighborhoods and creative cuisine.

Transport The L and J/M/Z lines serve North Brooklyn. The 2/3/, 4/5, A/C, B/D/F and N/Q/R serve South Brooklyn. The G connects north and south.

Getting around Walk, bike or ride the subway.

Tip Don't overlook lesser-known 'hoods like Bed-Stuy, Red Hook and Boerum Hill.

Wax poetic like Walt Whitman about the views from **Brooklyn Bridge Park** (p118).
🚶 7 min from High St station

Stroll down tree-shrouded sidewalks in **Brooklyn Heights** (p124), NYC's original suburb.
🚶 5 min from High St station

Brooklyn-Queens Expwy

BROOKLYN HEIGHTS

COBBLE HILL

Pay your respects to the famous residents at Gothic **Green-Wood Cemetery** (p130).
🚶 3 min from 25th St station

25th Ave
Ⓢ

4th Ave   Fifth Ave

Ⓢ 36th St

GREENPOINT

East River

Get your foodie fill at the **Smorgasburg** (p131) outdoor market.
🚶 *8 min from Bedford Ave station*

Order a flight at one of the **craft breweries** (p126) central to Williamsburg's booming beer scene.
🚶 *15 min from Bedford Ave station*

Snap photos of **street art** (p130) on blocks surrounding the Bushwick Collective.
🚶 *14 min from Morgan Ave station*

N 10th St

Kent Ave

Ⓢ Bedford Ave

WILLIAMSBURG

Graham Ave Ⓢ

Grand St Ⓢ

Grand St

Williamsburg Bridge

Broadway

Brooklyn-Queens Expwy

Dance till you drop at the **House of Yes** (p128) in Bushwick.
🚶 *12 min from Morgan Ave station*

Flushing Ave

Ⓢ Jefferson St

BUSHWICK

DUMBO

Brooklyn Bridge

Ⓢ High St
Ⓢ Clark St

Flatbush Ave

FORT GREENE

CLINTON HILL

Bedford Ave

Fulton St

Ⓢ Fulton St

Atlantic Ave

Lafayette Ave

BROOKLYN

Atlantic Ave Ⓢ

Join the borough's cultured class for a show at **Brooklyn Academy of Music** (p130).
🚶 *5 min from Atlantic Ave-Barclays Center station*

Grand Army Plaza Ⓢ

CROWN HEIGHTS

Eastern Pkwy-Brooklyn Museum Ⓢ

Skip through the sylvan landscape at **Prospect Park** (p130).
🚶 *5 min from Grand Army Plaza station*

Ⓢ Prospect Ave

PARK SLOPE

Prospect Park W

Flatbush Ave

Prospect Park

Prospect Pkwy

Ⓢ 15th St-Prospect Park

Ⓢ Prospect Park

N

0 ___ 1 mile
0 ___ 2 km

20 Sights & Sounds in
THE PARK

WATERFRONT | VIEWS | MODERN

If Brooklyn Bridge Park were an album, it'd be titled 'New York's Greatest Hits.' Views, history, arts venues and inspired cuisine – all in 85 acres of winding paths and piers stretching along the East River, making this recently revived urban oasis the consummate site for a quintessential New York afternoon.

🗺 How To

Getting here A/C to High St station, 2/3 to Clark St station, or F to York St station. For a grand entrance, walk over the Brooklyn Bridge from Manhattan.

When to go The views are great year-round, but the outdoor activities are best between May and October.

Top tip If walking across the Brooklyn Bridge on the weekend, go in the morning or evening to beat the crowds.

Warehouses Reimagined

It's nearly impossible to imagine that this prime real estate was ever undesirable, but beneath the park's carpet of green lies a complicated past. In the mid-19th century, Brooklyn became known as 'The Walled City' due to an impressive red-brick barrier formed by bustling warehouses lining the East River. By the 1970s, the businesses left, and the waterfront became a wasteland.

Today, the remnants of Brooklyn's industrial age have been revamped as trendy commercial destinations. **Empire Stores**, built between 1868 and 1885, once housed international goods like coffee, sugar, molasses and wool. It's now home to the TimeOut food market and a series of high-end retail shops. **St Ann's Warehouse**, a theater venue in a former tobacco facility next door, attracts

🔭 Landmark Lookout

Statue of Liberty Look west to see this green goddess.

One World Trade Center Downtown's tallest building rises a symbolic 1776ft.

Empire State Building Spot this art deco icon in Midtown.

Manhattan Bridge The blue suspension bridge marks the park's northern boundary.

Brooklyn Bridge Brooklyn's regal Gothic entryway.

Above left Brooklyn Bridge Park
Above right Empire Stores
Left St Ann's Warehouse

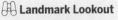

in-the-know New Yorkers with edgy plays and musical performances. Step inside the **Max Family Garden**, a connected outdoor nook, to see the space's industrial-chic makeover.

Anchors Away

Musical vessel Blaring ferry horns blend with Bach concertos on ***Bargemusic***, a turn-of-the-century coffee-bean barge transformed into a floating music hall. Walk the gangplank to hear classical concerts while rocking to the rhythms of the East River's waves. Events take place throughout the year at the foot of the Brooklyn Bridge.

Drinks on deck Slurp down oysters while sitting aboard the ***Pilot***, a century-old schooner docked at Pier 6. The seasonal boat-cum-restaurant serves alfresco food and drinks to an upscale Hamptons-style crowd from May to October.

Paddle for free Captain your own vessel by kayaking on the East River. Every summer,

Something for Everyone

Bike along the **Greenway**, watch your children play in the **WaterLab**, grill at the **Picnic Peninsula** and enjoy an ice-cream dessert. Stroll among public art installations and gardens, like the butterfly-filled **Flower Field** at Pier 6; learn about the local ecology at the Conservancy's **Education Center**; or watch the sun set behind the Statue of Liberty. Wrap your day with an array of dinner options and an evening program like Movies with a View or an acoustic concert set. The best days are the ones spent in Brooklyn Bridge Park.

By Eric Landau, *President, Brooklyn Bridge Park, Instagram* @brooklynbridgepark, *Twitter* @bbpnyc

Left **Brooklyn Bridge Park**
Below **Ample Hills Creamery**

the **Brooklyn Bridge Park Boathouse** offers free 20-minute paddle sessions so visitors can see Manhattan's silvery skyline while floating between Piers 1 and 2. Expect to see double-breasted cormorants and dabbling ducks joining your paddle party. These aquatic birds enjoy swimming along the shoreline year-round. Kayak times vary; reservations are mandatory.

Poetry in the Park

Stand on the wooden deck at **Fulton Ferry Landing** to see New York from the point of view of Walt Whitman, one of Brooklyn's greatest bards. Lines from 'Crossing Brooklyn Ferry,' his 1856 poem about riding a passenger boat from this spot to Manhattan, are inscribed on the guard rails as a love letter to the city's contemporary seafarers. Look out onto the same 'crested and scallop edg'd waves' that once entranced this queer, beard-wearing bohemian and consider how he might fare at a modern-day poetry slam in Bushwick.

Once your 'baffled and curious brain' is satisfied, continue to whet your Whitman appetite at **Ample Hills Creamery**, an ice-cream shop located in a former fireboat station beneath the Brooklyn Bridge. The company named itself after one of the poem's most famous lines: '...Brooklyn of ample hills was mine.'

Highway with a View

A COMPLICATED LOOK AT BROOKLYN'S BEST VISTA

New York City's perpetual state of reinvention might be awe-inspiring, but for every skyscraper built or roadway erected, something else meets its demise. This complex reality of urban planning crashes head-first on a Brooklyn expressway, where a prized park and a problematic thoroughfare are inextricably intertwined.

Standing on the **Brooklyn Heights Promenade** is a cinematic experience. On one side, Manhattan's modern skyscrapers shine like steely mountains; on the other, elegant townhomes conjure images of 19th-century domesticity. The panorama is so mesmerizing it's possible to forget there's a three-level highway flowing underneath.

This is the **Brooklyn-Queens Expressway** (BQE) – an 11.7-mile thoroughfare stretching from Brooklyn-Battery Tunnel near Red Hook to Grand Central Parkway in Queens. As the road snakes past Brooklyn Heights, it becomes a fantastic feat of urban design, seamlessly blending three tiers of traffic with a peaceful public esplanade.

But Brooklyn Heights Promenade is only 1826ft long. To say the rest of the BQE provides peace of any kind is laughable. The cement river floods into six lanes either side of the promenade and slices through the borough like a knife, carving Red Hook from Carroll Gardens, dicing Dumbo from downtown Brooklyn, cutting across the heart of Williamsburg, and leaving a gash near Greenpoint.

This massive roadway was part of urban planner Robert Moses' manifesto to drive NYC into what he saw as a car-fueled future. And Moses, who held a laundry list of unelected public offices from 1924 to 1968, seldom hit a red light while pushing his plans toward the finish line.

'You can draw any kind of picture you want on a clean slate and indulge your every whim in the wilderness in laying out a New Delhi, Canberra, or Brasilia,' he said, 'but when you operate in an overbuilt metropolis, you have to hack your way with a meat ax.'

Moses was a developer of biblical proportions who parted the city like the Red Sea for his cement machinations.

Left and right Brooklyn-Queens Expressway **Middle** Brooklyn Heights Promenade

It's nearly impossible to travel around New York without riding on his roads. During his tenure, he built at least 416 miles of parkways and seven bridges within New York City alone.

The construction of these new roads often meant the destruction of entire communities. Moses displaced roughly a quarter of a million New Yorkers in the name of urban renewal, tearing through neighborhoods primarily occupied by poor immigrants and people of color without the power to stand up to a political Goliath.

> Robert Moses displaced roughly a quarter of a million New Yorkers in the name of urban renewal.

But when Moses announced a plan to barrel the BQE down Hicks St, Brooklyn Heights' affluent White residents begged him to run it along the East River instead. Although this would lead to waterfront wreckage, it would spare most of the community's historic homes. Columbia Heights residents – who lived along the suggested route – went a step further, asking for a deck over the road to replace private gardens they would lose during construction. Moses agreed, but with one minor adjustment: the private gardens would become a park for the people. In 1950 Brooklyn Heights Promenade opened to the public.

Whether this beloved walkway is a gift from an unlikely Robin Hood or a devious form of highway robbery, one indisputable truth remains – nothing beats the view.

📖 Scenes from San Juan Hill

The thorny legacy of Robert Moses isn't always as visible as a six-lane expressway – unless you know where to look. Lincoln Center, Manhattan's elite arts institution, sits on top of what used to be known as San Juan Hill – an area occupied by African American and Puerto Rican New Yorkers until the mid-20th century. Moses razed the neighborhood as part of his federally funded 'slum clearance' initiative, displacing 7000 families and 800 businesses – but not before the 1961 movie adaptation of *West Side Story* had a chance to film parts of the opening sequence on its streets.

Walk Brooklyn's
HISTORY

HISTORY | ARCHITECTURE | STROLLING

▬▬▬ If the stately town houses of Brooklyn Heights could talk, they'd tell tales of scandalous pastors and bohemian poets; of filthy-rich merchants and former brothels. This King County enclave is a crowning achievement of historic preservation, with over 600 homes predating the Civil War. Uncover stories of bygone New York by strolling through Brooklyn's oldest neighborhood.

🕮 Trip Notes

Getting here/around Take the 2/3/4/5 to Borough Hall station and explore on foot.

When to go Walk around at dusk to see sumptuous brownstone interiors before wealthy residents draw their curtains for the evening, then head to the Brooklyn Heights Promenade for unobstructed sunset views.

Shop and eat Walk along the neighborhood's Atlantic Ave border for an outstanding selection of local restaurants, bars and boutiques.

🏛 Plymouth Church

From its pulpit in the 1850s and '60s, minister Henry Ward Beecher thundered forth to packed pews with outspoken abolitionist sermons. He opened the church's basement as a station on the Underground Railroad and held mock slave auctions during which the congregation would purchase the freedom of actual slaves.

By Tom Meyers, *co-host of Bowery Boys Podcast, which covers NYC history*

05 Peer at historic homes along the 'Fruit Streets' (Pineapple, Cranberry and Orange) until you reach the Federal-style house at **24 Middagh St** (1824).

Middagh St

Willow St

Orange St

Hicks St

S High St

Plymouth Church

Orange St

BROOKLYN HEIGHTS

04 In the 1950s, Truman Capote wrote *In Cold Blood, Breakfast at Tiffany's* and a passionate valentine to Brooklyn Heights while living at **70 Willow St** (1899).

Pineapple St

03 From the 1920s through the 1970s, the **Hotel St George** (1885–1929) was a cruising site for gay men, including poet Hart Crane and playwright Tennessee Williams.

S Clark St

Henry St

01 Admire the terra-cotta ornaments adorning the Queen Anne–style exterior of the **Center for Brooklyn History** (1881) before perusing the exhibitions inside.

02 The Romanesque Revival **Herman Behr Mansion** (1888) has changed from single-family home to hotel, to brothel, to Franciscan monk residence, to apartment complex.

Pierrepont St

Clinton St

N 0 ——————— 200 m
0 ——————— 0.1 miles

JON BILOUS/ALAMY STOCK PHOTO ©,
TATIANATATIANATATIANA/SHUTTERSTOCK ©

S Court St

22 Williamsburg Craft-Beer
CRAWL

LOCAL | TAPROOMS | NIGHTLIFE

Williamsburg's heady history as a beer hub dates back to the 19th century, but it wasn't until the emergence of Brooklyn Brewery in 1996 that the Burg began its ascension to microbrew mecca. Now, the neighborhood is awash with craft-beer chemists. Join hophead hipsters soaking up suds in some of the borough's hottest taprooms.

🍺 **Beer Borough**

Try locally brewed beer in nearby neighborhoods:

Strong Rope Brewery (Gowanus; pictured)

Fifth Hammer (Long Island City)

KCBC (Bushwick)

Wild East Brewing Co (Gowanus)

🗺 **Trip Notes**

Getting here Take the L between Bedford, Lorimer and Grand stations unless you want to explore the neighborhood on foot.

When to go Most working taprooms open in the afternoon and close around midnight.

Top tip Order flights instead of pints so you can sample more flavors without over-imbibing. Bring home a growler once you find your favorite beer.

By Christopher Gandsy, *owner, chef and brewer, Daleview Biscuits and Beer in Prospect Lefferts Gardens, @biscuitsandbeer*

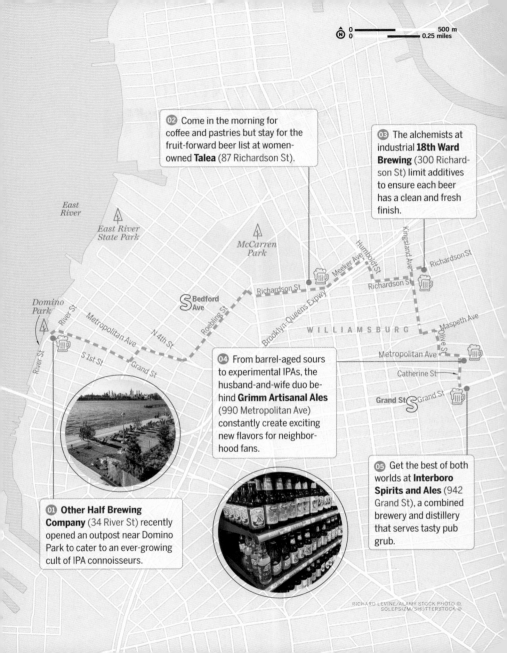

02 Come in the morning for coffee and pastries but stay for the fruit-forward beer list at women-owned **Talea** (87 Richardson St).

03 The alchemists at industrial **18th Ward Brewing** (300 Richardson St) limit additives to ensure each beer has a clean and fresh finish.

04 From barrel-aged sours to experimental IPAs, the husband-and-wife duo behind **Grimm Artisanal Ales** (990 Metropolitan Ave) constantly create exciting new flavors for neighborhood fans.

05 Get the best of both worlds at **Interboro Spirits and Ales** (942 Grand St), a combined brewery and distillery that serves tasty pub grub.

01 **Other Half Brewing Company** (34 River St) recently opened an outpost near Domino Park to cater to an ever-growing cult of IPA connoisseurs.

East River

East River State Park

McCarren Park

Domino Park

Bedford Ave

WILLIAMSBURG

River St

Metropolitan Ave

N 4th St

Roebling St

Richardson St

Brooklyn-Queens Expwy

Meeker Ave

Humboldt St

Kingsland Ave

Richardson St

Richardson St

Maspeth Ave

Metropolitan Ave

Catherine St

Grand St

Grand St

S 1st St

Grand St

0 | 500 m
0 | 0.25 miles

23 Party in North
BROOKLYN

CLUBS | DANCING | MUSIC

When the city that doesn't sleep wants to dance until dawn, it heads to a warehouse in North Brooklyn. These once-abandoned buildings have become the prime settings for East Williamsburg and Bushwick's transformation into a modern Weimar Berlin, where all are welcome and anything goes.

📖 How To

Getting here/around Take the L to Montrose Ave station for East Williamsburg, or Jefferson St station for Bushwick. The area is covered in street art and worth walking around.

When to go Weekend nights are best. Check websites for an event that tickles your fancy.

Plan ahead Book tickets in advance to ensure admittance. Arrive early to avoid queues.

Glitter explosion Burning Man meets Moulin Rouge at **House of Yes**, an ice factory turned arts temple that throws inclusive and wild events in Bushwick. Performances by aerialists, magicians and burlesque dancers set the mood for an eclectic crowd of attendees, who sport psychedelic DIY costumes to themed shindigs. This club isn't the kind of place where you wear a T-shirt and jeans unless they're bedazzled and dipped in glitter.

Queer brew It might be hard to imagine while twirling on **3 Dollar Bill**'s massive outdoor dance floor, but Brooklyn's

Top right Elsewhere
Bottom right Avant Gardner

🕺 How to House of Yes

Dress in something that makes you feel happy and fabulous. Wear your most comfortable, bad-ass dancing shoes. Party with a purpose and set a positive intention: your energy can make someone else's night more amazing. Stick around until 3:45am, when the infamous Last Call Pizza announces closing time by dancing around the bar in a pizza suit.

By Kae Burke, co-founder and Creative Director, House of Yes, @kaeburke

biggest queer club was once the site of lager maker Otto Huber Brewery. Now, this East Williamsburg megaplex throws circuit parties, drag shows, flea markets and comedy nights.

Indie jams Sip cocktails on a rooftop as the sun sets over Bushwick, then explore the three-floor maze of venues. This is **Elsewhere**: a former furniture factory that hosts indie concerts, dance parties and immersive art shows.

EDM kingdom Avant Gardner's 80,000-sq-ft palace is an entire block with multiple venues. In summer, a central courtyard opens as Brooklyn Mirage, an outdoor dance-and-concert space with Manhattan skyline views.

Listings

BEST OF THE REST

🏞 Green Spaces

Prospect Park

Stroll, bike, picnic or play around this lush 585-acre landscape designed by the same architects behind Central Park. Don't miss free concerts at the Bandshell, skating at the LeFrak Center or paddling the perimeter of Prospect Park Lake.

McCarren Park

On warm weekends, this 35-acre park linking Williamsburg and Greenpoint is a people-watching paradise. Find a big family BBQ, an acoustic jam session and an organized sport event before jumping in the public pool.

Green-Wood Cemetery

A 19th-century graveyard with 478 acres of snaking paths, Gothic mausoleums and arresting Manhattan views. Nearly 600,000 New Yorkers, including Leonard Bernstein and Jean-Michel Basquiat, call these hallowed grounds their forever home.

🎇 Annual Festivals

Afropunk Festival

Every August, this multi-genre music festival brings artists like Janelle Monae and Big Freedia to Commodore Barry Park for a week-end of live performances, funky fashion, craft markets and food trucks.

Bushwick Collective Block Party

World-renowned street artists paint new murals on walls near Troutman St and St Nicholas Ave in the days leading up to this joyous June celebration featuring art, food and live music.

Dyker Heights Christmas Lights

Between Thanksgiving and New Year's Eve, no neighborhood shines brighter than Dyker Heights. Walk around masterfully lit lawns of single-family homes to see the ostentatious holiday display.

🎭 Performing Arts & Museums

Brooklyn Academy of Music (BAM)

BAM is the cultural heart of Kings County with multiple venues showcasing a mix of groundbreaking plays, revered dance troupes, classical operas and indie films.

Brooklyn Museum

This 19th-century beaux-arts museum near Prospect Park boasts a collection spanning 1.5 million objects. Expect to see everything from ancient Egyptian mummies to 21st-century masterpieces.

New York Transit Museum

Learn stories about NYC's mass transit system while climbing aboard vintage trains inside this subterranean subway station from the 1930s.

☕ Coffee & Confections

Sey Coffee $

The bright, minimalist decor helps highlight what's most important at this Brooklyn-based micro-roastery: really good coffee. Here, a shot of espresso is like a glass of fine wine.

Devoción $

Sip fresh Colombian coffee while lounging on a tufted leather sofa in this local chain's industrial-chic Williamsburg location.

Fan-Fan Doughnuts $

If a fan-fan is the dough baby of an éclair and a Long John, this Bed-Stuy shop is their bakery obstetrician. Try flavors like guava and cheese, yuzu meringue and miso cider glaze.

Four and Twenty Blackbirds $

There are two locations for this homemade pie purveyor, but Prospect Heights is best if you want to wash down a slice of Salty Honey with wine, beer or cold brew.

International Cuisine

Lilia $$$

This former auto body shop is now a pasta parlor that churns out tasty handmade noodles. The adjoining Lilia Caffé serves coffee and sweets.

Xilonen $$

Tastefully made and artfully plated Mexican food that's mostly vegan. Order a cocktail, try a tostada and kick back in the stylish space for brunch or dinner.

La Vara $$$

Spanish tapas with Jewish and Moorish influences served in an intimate exposed-brick dining room. The adjoining cafe is equally charming, as is nearby Cobble Hill Park.

Bunna Cafe $$

Wash your hands before eating at this cozy Bushwick joint – you'll be using them while digging into heaping platters of plant-based Ethiopian classics with soft and tangy injera flatbread.

Ursula $

In-the-know chile fiends queue up early for New Mexican–style breakfast burritos, served until noon from Wednesday through Sunday at this colorful cafe and bakery.

A&A Bake Doubles and Roti $

An unassuming Bed-Stuy institution famous for authentic Trinidadian snacks like doubles, where deep-fried dough is wrapped around a curried chickpea concoction.

Bolero $$

Farm-fresh, family-style Vietnamese dishes that fall somewhere between casual cuisine and fine dining. This sleek, contemporary restaurant is umami personified.

Classy Cocktails

Elsa $$

Slip into a U-shaped booth at this art deco bar to enjoy expertly crafted cocktails and beer poured from a Singer sewing machine. Don't leave without using the loo – bathroom-mirror selfies are mandatory.

Maison Premiere $$

Raw oysters and enough absinthe to ignite a new era of Impressionism are the main reasons to visit this vintage bar with Toulouse-Lautrec allure.

Trendy Markets

Artists and Fleas Williamsburg

Vintage clothes, handmade jewelry, and clocks made from hardcover classics are a few of the items sold by Brooklyn-based creatives at this hip Williamsburg marketplace. Weekends only.

Smorgasburg

Weekly open-air food bazaar with four NYC outposts. Stop by Williamsburg's East River location on Saturdays to sample hand-held goodies served by dozens of local vendors. Open spring through autumn.

Scan to find more things to do in Brooklyn online

EAST VILLAGE & THE LOWER EAST SIDE

CULTURE | ART | HISTORY

Experience the East Village & the Lower East Side online

EAST VILLAGE & THE LOWER EAST SIDE
Trip Builder

TAKE YOUR PICK OF MUST-SEES AND HIDDEN GEMS

The East Village and Lower East Side neighborhoods are home to the best of New York City's creative counterculture. Whether you're up for a vintage rock venue, open-mike poetry slam, quirky museum, offbeat restaurant with shockingly excellent food, or even a spontaneous tattoo, this neighborhood has you covered.

Neighborhood Notes

Best for A fun night out, museum-hopping, delicious dining, counterculture.

Transport L to First Ave station, 6 to Astor Place station, F to Second Ave station.

Getting around Explore on foot or by bike.

Tip Houston St is the 'dividing line' between East Village and Lower East Side.

Union Square

14th St-Union Sq — E 14th St — 3rd Ave

Indulge in some gourmet snacks and desserts at **Union Square Green Market** (p141).
🚶 1 min from 14th St-Union Sq station

8th St-NYU — Astor Pl

Washington Square Park

Broadway — Lafayette St — Fourth Ave — Cooper Square

See a local rock band play at the iconic **Bowery Ballroom** (p137).
🚶 10 min from Second Ave station

NOLITA

Kenmare St

Broadway — Centre St

Canal St

Canal St — LITTLE ITALY

Canal St

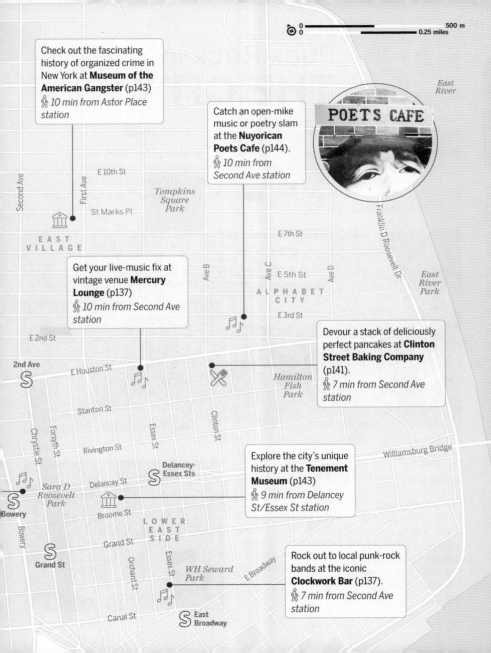

Check out the fascinating history of organized crime in New York at **Museum of the American Gangster** (p143)
🚶 *10 min from Astor Place station*

Catch an open-mike music or poetry slam at the **Nuyorican Poets Cafe** (p144).
🚶 *10 min from Second Ave station*

POETS CAFE

Get your live-music fix at vintage venue **Mercury Lounge** (p137)
🚶 *10 min from Second Ave station*

Devour a stack of deliciously perfect pancakes at **Clinton Street Baking Company** (p141).
🚶 *7 min from Second Ave station*

Explore the city's unique history at the **Tenement Museum** (p143)
🚶 *9 min from Delancey St/Essex St station*

Rock out to local punk-rock bands at the iconic **Clockwork Bar** (p137).
🚶 *7 min from Second Ave station*

East River

East River Park

EAST VILLAGE

ALPHABET CITY

LOWER EAST SIDE

Tompkins Square Park

Hamilton Fish Park

Sara D Roosevelt Park

WH Seward Park

Williamsburg Bridge

Second Ave
First Ave
E 10th St
St Marks Pl
E 7th St
Ave B
Ave C
Ave D
E 5th St
E 3rd St
E 2nd St
Franklin D Roosevelt Dr
E Houston St
2nd Ave
Stanton St
Chrystie St
Forsyth St
Essex St
Clinton St
Rivington St
Delancey-Essex Sts
Delancey St
Bowery
Broome St
Grand St
Grand St
Orchard St
Essex St
E Broadway
Canal St
East Broadway

0 500 m
0 0.25 miles

24 Punk Rock in
THE CITY

CULTURE | HISTORY | MUSIC

The Annual Punk Rock Riot Reunion Show takes place every first weekend of August in Tompkins Square Park to commemorate a 1988 riot to protest a park-wide curfew. Locals, activists, youths and more gather to enjoy a punk-rock show from the best local bands. It's a must-see, and the East Village at its most authentic and fun!

🗺 How To

Getting here L to First Ave station, exiting on the Ave A side. Tompkins Square Park is just a few blocks away.

When to go The concert is usually from 2pm to 6pm on the first Saturday and Sunday of every August.

What to wear August is hot and humid. Dress light and prepare to sweat!

Make it fashion Wear your most fun, outlandish punk-rock gear, show off your tattoos, mohawk your hair – anything goes!

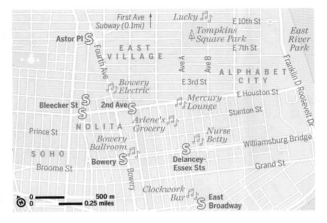

First Ave ↑
Subway (0.1mi)
Astor Pl
Lucky 🎵
E 10th St
Tompkins
Square Park
East
River
Park
E 7th St
E A S T
V I L L A G E
Fourth Ave
Ave A
Ave B
A L P H A B E T
C I T Y
Bowery
Electric 🎵
E 3rd St
Franklin D Roosevelt Dr
Bleecker St
2nd Ave
Mercury
Lounge 🎵
E Houston St
Stanton St
Prince St
N O L I T A
Arlene's 🎵
Grocery
Nurse
Betty 🎵
Williamsburg Bridge
S O H O
Bowery
Ballroom 🎵
Bowery 🎵
Delancey-
Essex Sts
Grand St
Broome St
Bowery
Clockwork
Bar 🎵
East
Broadway
0 — 500 m
0 — 0.25 miles

Top left Arlene's Grocery
Bottom left Bowery Electric

🎧 **Riot Act**

The organizers of the **Annual Punk Rock Riot** put on seven shows a season at various locations throughout NYC and the East Village. We do it for the people. We've been putting on punk-rock shows for 33 years since the first riot in Tompkins Square Park. If you visit the East Village in the summer, you'll find us.

The best part about punk music in the East Village is that it brings the community together. It also keeps punk rock from the '70s and '80s alive and passes it on to the next generation. We see kids and teenagers showing up and loving the music like we did when we were their age – it keeps alive the counterculture that flourished in the East Village and on the Lower East Side before gentrification came along.

By Chris Flash, *activist, journalist and organizer of punk-rock concerts in Tompkins Square Park and the Annual Punk Rock Riot Show*

Music Venues of the East Village & Lower East Side

Live music is the heart and soul of the East Village and the Lower East Side. As the birthplace of punk rock and host to some of the city's best dive bars, this neighborhood scene is truly not to be missed. The Bowery, once home to the legendary now-closed venue CBGB, has become the landing place for a plethora of excellent live-music venues hosting the city's and the world's best acts. **Bowery Electric** (theboweryelectric. com) has two floors and drinks a-flowing almost every night of the week. The owners are lifelong rock-and-roll fanatics and are passionate about keeping the vibe alive in the East Village and beyond. **Bowery Ballroom** (mercuryeastpresents.com) also hosts multiple live bands per week, as does its sister venue Mercury Lounge a short walk away. Mercury Lounge launched the careers of top bands like the Strokes, Interpol and the Yeah Yeah Yeahs, while Bowery Ballroom has hosted Patti Smith, Lou Reed and Kanye West.

Now a clothing store, the old **CBGB** venue where the Ramones played their first major shows in 1974 – and the official birthplace of the NYC punk scene – can be found at 315 Bowery. This is a quintessential nostalgic and historical walk-by for posterity's sake. The punk, grunge and dive scene lives on at a number of must-visit, lively venues such as **Clockwork Bar**, which has a famously cheap $5-beer-and-a-shot special, as well as **Arlene's Grocery** and **Nurse Betty**. The woman-owned **Lucky** bar also warrants a friendly stop-in.

ROLINDUST/GETTY IMAGES ©

Punk Is Not Dead

PUNK ROCKS ON IN THE CITY OF ITS BIRTH

The world's first punk band, the Ramones, formed as a group of wayward NYC teenagers in 1974. At the time, the East Village was home to the famous CBGB, the first venue to put them on stage, instantly making the entire neighborhood a living museum of punk-rock history.

In the early months of 1974, four middle-class teenagers from Queens, New York City, joined together to form what would become the first official punk-rock band in music history – the Ramones. Searching desperately for a fresh, hard-edged departure from the flower-child, hippie-music era of the '60s, the youth of New York were growing restless. After peaking with Jimi Hendrix' incomparable genius, the era of long, drawn-out guitar solos was quickly fading. It was just at this moment in 1974 when punk rock crashed into town, bringing the breathless, stripped down, anti-establishment sound that the world needed.

The Ramones' first official show occurred at Performance Studios, followed by a first booking at the soon-to-be-legendary CBGB on the Bowery in the East Village. With their distinctly anti-hippie look – choppy hair, ripped clothes, black leather jackets and worn-out boots – a new and glamorously chaotic world was born. Soon, a punk scene began to grow rapidly around CBGB, which began hosting the genre's hottest acts, including Patti Smith, Suicide, Television and Blondie. The new sound was such an instant, riotous hit in New York City that the Ramones would play an astounding 74 shows from their first show in August 1974 through to the end of the year. Other bars and clubs quickly began to open their doors to the new sound, including legends such as Fillmore East on Second Ave and Café Au Go Go on Bleecker St.

The youth of New York had created an entirely new and original approach to making music. The East Village and Lower East Side had always been home to New York City's counterculture, but by the end of the '70s it was punk rock against the world. Before each set, Dee Dee Ramone

Left Sign for Joey Ramone Pl, East Village **Middle** CBGB, pictured before it closed in 2006 **Right** Musician, Central Park

would shout a messy rapid-fire count of '1-2-3-4' followed by a series of short, staccato, rough-edged songs – often consisting of the same three chords underneath loud, political lyrics. It was the ultimate novelty. Rock critics at the time didn't know how to wrap their heads around such an extraordinarily new phenomenon, much less describe it in words or in print. The movement itself was happening on stage in real time: the magic of the moment could only be found in the chords and songs themselves. Every night was more ephemeral than the next. Critics struggled to capture that level of pure zeitgeist even if they tried. Every night on the Bowery in the East Village, something new burst into life and a piece of the old died. The movement spread across the pond with lightning speed and UK bands like the Clash and the Sex Pistols took the punk-rock sound to new heights. By the end of the 1970s and moving into the 1980s, punk rock was global and thriving.

Four teenagers from Queens, New York City, with a thirst for something new had played an unforgettable show at CBGB in the East Village, and the world was never the same.

> The East Village and Lower East Side had always been home to New York City's counterculture, but by the end of the '70s it was punk rock against the world.

♫♪ Live-Music Capital

New York is known for some of the finest music venues in the world, as well as for a thriving bar scene with hundreds of live-music options. Whether you're interested in rock, classical, jazz, electronic, reggae or experimental music, there's a place for everyone. But what is the unspoken best live-music venue in New York? The street! Some of the finest orchestral musicians from the renowned Juilliard School, Carnegie Hall and Lincoln Center will spontaneously set up solo shows in Central Park or a corner of their choosing – solely to share their art with fellow New Yorkers.

25

Delis, Doughnuts
& DINING

FOOD | CULTURE | MARKETS

New York City is famous for its delicious bagel shops, delis, eclectic food markets, green grocers with fresh produce and so much more. The East Village and the Lower East Side, in particular, host some of the top delis, stop-in shops and bagel joints in town. Read along to get your snack on with the downtown locals.

ROBERT K. CHIN - STOREFRONTS/ALAMY STOCK PHOTO ©

🗺 How To

Getting here F to Second Ave station, or the F/M, J/Z to Delancey St-Essex St station.

When to go Spring, summer and fall are the best times to peruse these neighborhoods for tasty treats.

Tip Favorites like Katz's Deli and Russ & Daughters are popular with both tourists and locals, meaning lines can stretch around the block. Visit outside traditional breakfast, lunch and dinner rush hours for best results.

ELEANOR LEE/SHUTTERSTOCK ©

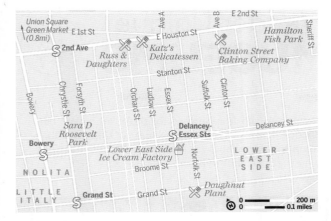

Top left Clinton Street Baking Company **Bottom left** Doughnuts from Doughnut Plant

Snack Attack

Pancakes, doughnuts and sweets On any given day in New York City, you'll spend countless amounts of time walking. Even after exiting the subway, you usually have to walk a few blocks or more to your destination. Capturing those potentially hungry consumers, fresh off the subway en route to their destinations, is a New York deli and bakery specialty. In that short walk from the train, dozens of phenomenal places to grab a snack will intentionally appear before you. **Doughnut Plant** on the Lower East Side is one of the best places to snack, complete with regular specials and vegan and even gluten-free options. **Clinton Street Baking Company** on Houston St has you covered for all of your pancake needs – be sure to try the lemon ricotta pancakes – and **Lower East Side Ice Cream Factory** at Essex Market is the big summer winner.

Bagels, pastrami sandwiches and lox On the savory side, **Katz's Delicatessen**, a local and national favorite established in 1888, serves up some of the finest deli specialties in the city. Its pastrami-on-rye sandwich is famous, as is its corned beef and various potato and egg salads. Fourth-generation family-owned deli **Russ & Daughters**, a stone's throw away and also on Houston St, is home to a legendary bagel and epic smoked-fish selection. Both delis are top-tier experiences.

🏛 Union Square Green Market

Union Square Green Market on the north corner of Union Square Park is the best open-air fruit, vegetable, flower, bread and specialty-item market in NYC. Originally starting with just a few farmers back in 1976, the now world-famous market often peaks at over 140 seasonal and regional farmers. Over 60,000 shoppers are known to come through the market on any given day, and entertaining cooking demonstrations, live music and tastings abound. The best part is this market isn't only reserved for weekends, but also takes place on Mondays and Wednesdays when it's less crowded. Book signings organized by the incredible **Food Book Fair** (foodbookfair.com) are scheduled on Saturdays from May to November.

26 Wander Unique MUSEUMS

ART | CULTURE | MUSEUMS

New York City's museums are world renowned for their vast collections and high standard of excellence. The lesser-known museums of the East Village and Lower East Side maintain that same high standard but offer a delightfully local and offbeat downtown experience not to be missed.

ROBERT K. CHIN - STOREFRONTS/ALAMY STOCK PHOTO ©

🗺 How To

Getting here J/Z train to Bowery station.

When to go Tenement Museum is only open Thursday to Tuesday.

Seasonal crowds NYC's tourism season is lengthy, sometimes lasting year-round. When in doubt, visit on a weekday for smaller crowds.

What to wear Wear comfortable sneakers for walking between museums and for potential walking tours.

Pricing Museum of the American Gangster ($15), Tenement Museum ($30), New Museum ($18).

LEWIS TSE PUI LUNG/SHUTTERSTOCK ©

Top left Tenement Museum
Bottom left New Museum

Distinctive Downtown Museums

New Museum This gem on the Bowery is the only museum in New York City devoted entirely to contemporary art. The museum was founded rather recently in 1977 and was created specifically to give less-recognized avant-garde artists the same opportunities for critical evaluation and international visibility as major artists. This is a knock-out experience to be remembered.

Tenement Museum Unlike most museums that hold paintings by great masters or fantastical contemporary installations, Tenement Museum is full of keepsakes that tell the incredible stories of real people living real lives as first-generation Americans in New York City. A spool of thread and a pair of scissors from the 1800s tell the story of a blue-collar seamstress in Little Italy, while a deck of cards and black-and-white photos from the Great Depression tell four generations' worth of stories from a Lower East Side family. This museum is a diamond worth uncovering.

Museum of the American Gangster Located on St Mark's Place in the East Village, this tiny two-room museum in a former speakeasy is the ultimate niche experience in the neighborhood. Collections explore the history of organized crime in New York City and how it shaped culture, myth and memory. Photographs, drawings and other quirky memorabilia of the most famous American gangsters will have visitors thoroughly entertained.

✖️ Eats Near the Arts

After a long day of museum-going, grab a bite to eat at a local snack shop, wine bar or restaurant. The Tenement Museum is conveniently located on the Lower East Side and favorites like Katz's Deli and Clinton Street Baking Company are close by. The New Museum is just a stone's throw from **Lombardi's** on Spring St, the oldest pizzeria in the country. The Museum of the American Gangster has Lucky close by on Ave B, where you can stop in for a beer and a snack.

By Amanda Dell, *Program Director, Jewish Food Society and host of the 'Schmaltzy' podcast, @amanda_dell*

27 How to Spend
A DAY

MUSEUMS | MUSIC | CULTURE

▬▬▬ A satisfying day in the East Village and Lower East Side will take you on a rollercoaster ride you will never forget. Whether strolling through this neighborhood's upbeat park, grabbing a bagel from its best deli, or catching a live music show offering the best in local bands, this walk will be the ride of your life!

NIELSKLIIM/SHUTTERSTOCK ©

🞷 Open-Mike Nights

Open-mike nights where you can perform your own music, poetry and comedy are popular and easy to find in the East Village and Lower East Side.

Nuyorican Poets Cafe (nuyorican.org)

Bowery Poetry Club (bowerypoetry.com)

Otto's Shrunken Head (ottos shrunkenhead.com)

Parkside Lounge (parksidelounge.nyc)

KGB Bar (kgbbar.com)

📖 Trip Notes

Getting around L to 14th St station and walk to Aves A and B. F to Second Ave station and walk to Aves A and B.

When to go Open-mike nights usually fall on weekdays. Check websites.

Get creative If you attend an open-mike, feel free to jump on stage! Everyone is welcome and first-timers are always supported.

Must-see streets 8th St between Second and Third Aves, known as St Mark's Place.

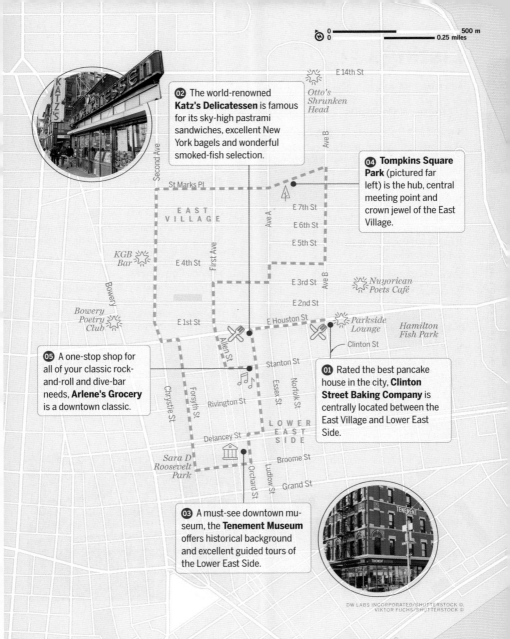

02 The world-renowned **Katz's Delicatessen** is famous for its sky-high pastrami sandwiches, excellent New York bagels and wonderful smoked-fish selection.

04 **Tompkins Square Park** (pictured far left) is the hub, central meeting point and crown jewel of the East Village.

05 A one-stop shop for all of your classic rock-and-roll and dive-bar needs, **Arlene's Grocery** is a downtown classic.

01 Rated the best pancake house in the city, **Clinton Street Baking Company** is centrally located between the East Village and Lower East Side.

03 A must-see downtown museum, the **Tenement Museum** offers historical background and excellent guided tours of the Lower East Side.

E 14th St

Otto's Shrunken Head

Ave B

St Marks Pl

EAST VILLAGE

E 7th St
E 6th St
E 5th St

Ave A

KGB Bar

E 4th St

First Ave

Second Ave

E 3rd St
Ave B

Nuyorican Poets Café

E 2nd St

Bowery

Bowery Poetry Club

E 1st St

E Houston St

Parkside Lounge

Hamilton Fish Park

Clinton St

Allen St

Stanton St

Chrystie St

Forsyth St

Essex St

Norfolk St

Rivington St

LOWER EAST SIDE

Delancey St

Sara D Roosevelt Park

Orchard St

Ludlow St

Broome St

Grand St

500 m
0.25 miles

Listings

BEST OF THE REST

☕ Coffee & Cocktails

Ninth Street Espresso $

This consistently top-rated coffeehouse is a neighborhood staple. It has two locations: the original at 9th St and Ave C, and the other on 10th St between Aves A and B.

Mud Coffee $

A local favorite, Mud Coffee offers espresso with a one-of-a-kind flavor. It also has a charming backyard garden and a couch in front for catching up with friends.

Saltwater Coffee $

For Aussie visitors, this will be a welcome slice of home. This Australian-owned cafe has some of the best pastries and espresso in the neighborhood. Try the turmeric latte.

Kona Coffee and Company $

An excellent coffee shop, Kona offers strong espresso and an interesting Hawaiian vibe. Be sure to try the Hawaiian iced latte.

Amor y Amargo $$$

This cocktail bar is named Amargo after the word for 'bitter' in Spanish. It's the United States' first cocktail bar dedicated exclusively to bitters – Italian amari in particular.

p.d.t. $$

You can only enter this speakeasy through a mysterious phone booth located in the hot-dog joint next store. A dark room with impeccable drinks greets you on the other side.

Garret East $$

Visually this bar is very beautiful and the decor matches the quality of its strong, well-made cocktails. It's a great place to have a nightcap or after-dinner cocktail.

Death & Company $$

Despite its dark name, this bar is a fun, low-key spot with delicious cocktails made with excellent ingredients. The vodka and whiskey drinks really sing.

🚚 On-the-Go Eats

Mamoun's $

The falafel is the most famous item on the menu here and comes in both sandwich and platter styles. Items have fun nicknames like 'The East Village' and 'The West Village.'

Two Hands Corn Dogs $

This small shop doesn't serve traditional American hot dogs, but instead a delicious form of Korean corndog with spicy flavors and perfect chipotle mayonnaise.

Confectionary! $$

At this macaron oasis, sidestep the regular vanilla, chocolate and strawberry varieties and try instead the Earl Grey, lemon meringue or birthday-cake options. The special flavors rotate.

Mamoun's

LeVain Bakery $

A popular bakery located on the busy and bustling Lafayette St, Levain has epic soft-baked cookies. The best is the dark chocolate and peanut-butter flavor.

Ippudo $$

This minimalist well-appointed Japanese restaurant has stellar ramen. The staff yells out in Japanese at random intervals, welcoming new guests.

Tompkins Square Bagels $

A neighborhood staple with perfect bagels: firm and crunchy on the outside, soft on the inside. Also, cream cheese and lox options galore.

Black Seed Bagels $

You name it, you can get it on your bagel. Here anything that typically goes in a sandwich, can be added to your bagel.

Wine Bars

Ruffian $$$

This bar serves an enormously wide and delicious assortment of wines, including orange wines, natural wines and Georgian wines.

Corkbuzz $$$

The East Village version of this special wine bar has a great atmosphere. The lighting is impeccable and staff are knowledgeable.

Gnocco $$

A lovely, small wine bar on 10th St with wines from specific wineries on hand. Both the wines and the cuisine are delicious and specific to northern Italy's Emilia region.

Ten Bells $$

This favorite on the Lower East Side has a penchant for aromatic organic wines, oysters and interesting small plates.

Tompkins Square Bagels

Lena $$

Lena doubles as a classic wine bar and a full-service restaurant. It has a rustic-yet-elegant vibe and a French-leaning menu.

Bibi Wine Bar $$

A laid-back and casual wine bar with A+ food and beverages. Small plates, sandwiches and salads are plentiful.

Antler $$

Located on the Lower East Side, this wine bar also offers a nice selection of beer and small plates. The space is intimate and simple.

Thrift Stores

Cure Thrift Store

Cure is a must visit for anyone looking for a great outfit at a great price for a great cause. All proceeds go to juvenile diabetes research and advocacy efforts.

Housing Works

Known around the city for its quality second-hand clothes and furniture, Housing Works sometimes stocks one-of-a-kind pieces. Don't skip this one!

Scan to find more things to do in the East Village & the Lower East Side online

EAST VILLAGE & THE LOWER EAST SIDE REVIEWS

28 Tour Little Italy's Old **CATHEDRAL**

CULTURE | ART | CATHEDRAL

■■■■ Old St Patrick's Cathedral in Little Italy is the oldest cathedral in New York, and the city's only basilica. This little-known and very beautiful tour explores the catacombs underneath Little Italy as well as parts of the church and its history that are off-limits to regular visitors.

MASSIMILIANO BROGGI/ALAMY STOCK PHOTO ©

🗺 How To

When to go The tour is open year-round, but spring, summer and fall are best for walking through the neighborhood.

Getting here 6 to Bleecker St station, B/D to Grand St station.

Getting around Little Italy is best explored on foot.

Gelato kings In addition to great Italian restaurants, Little Italy has top-notch gelato. Grab one and see for yourself!

DAN HERRICK/LONELY PLANET ©

Far left Interior, Old St Patrick's Cathedral **Near left** Exterior, Old St Patrick's Cathedral **Bottom** Lombardi's

The 'Other' St Patrick's Cathedral

Most visitors to New York City are familiar with St Patrick's Cathedral, the beautiful church located on Fifth Ave and 51st St that sees hundred of thousands of locals and tourists per year. However, downtown in Little Italy, there is another smaller and older cathedral that was the original Cathedral of the Archdiocese of New York. It was constructed over 200 years ago in the heart of the neighborhood on Mott and Prince Sts and continues to be a central point. Locally called 'Old St Pat's,' this cathedral was seen as a lighthouse in the dark during some very dismal times in the once-impoverished Irish community that immigrated to the country in the 19th century.

A detailed tour is available that allows locals and tourists to explore the rich history of the cathedral through an exploration of its underground catacombs. The tour takes you through multiple years of New York history and, in particular, the history of the church. Best of all, the tour is conducted underground by candlelight, which adds a mysterious and enchanting element to the experience. The tour guides are all very experienced and the tour groups are kept small and manageable to help the guides connect with their guests.

Also check out the Museum of Chinese in the Americas on Centre St, a short walk away.

Little Italy at a Glance

The **San Gennaro Festival** happens every fall in Little Italy. It's a colorful festival, with foods, trinkets and activities that spill out onto the streets. Generally speaking, a stroll up and down Lafayette St is entertaining. Maybe stop in for dinner at **Ruby Rosa** or **Gelso & Grand** after your walk.

The second edition of the **MoMA Design Store** is also located down here over on Spring St. If you love pizza, stop by **Lombardi's**, which is officially the oldest pizzeria in the entire United States (1905). Its pizza is perfection!

By Keili FitzGerald, *professional photographer and artist, @KeiliFitzGerald*

UPPER EAST SIDE

MUSEUMS | RESTAURANTS | SHOPPING

Experience the Upper East Side online

UPPER EAST SIDE
Trip Builder

TAKE YOUR PICK OF MUST-SEES AND HIDDEN GEMS

▬▬▬ Known for being home to some of the city's wealthiest residents, the Upper East Side is often seen as the backdrop to movies and films focused on the top 1% of wealth. However, visitors will find more than million-dollar real estate in this quaint neighborhood, which has abundant boutiques, high-end restaurants and art galleries close to Central Park.

🕮 Neighborhood Notes

Best for Afternoon jaunts to museums, art galleries or shops.

Transport 4/5/6 trains along Lexington Ave. N/R/Q trains along Second Ave. Crosstown buses at 96th, 86th and 72nd Sts.

Getting around Most places are close to public transportation.

Tip Many businesses close at 8pm in the residential areas uptown from 86th St.

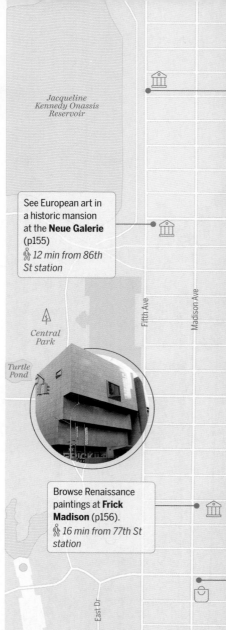

Jacqueline Kennedy Onassis Reservoir

See European art in a historic mansion at the **Neue Galerie** (p155)
🚶 12 min from 86th St station

Central Park

Fifth Ave

Madison Ave

Turtle Pond

Browse Renaissance paintings at **Frick Madison** (p156).
🚶 16 min from 77th St station

East Dr

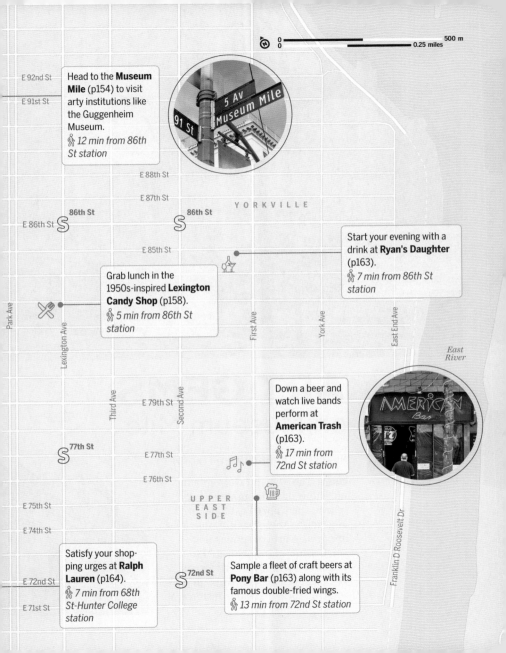

Head to the **Museum Mile** (p154) to visit arty institutions like the Guggenheim Museum.
🚶 12 min from 86th St station

5 AV
Museum Mile
91 St

E 92nd St
E 91st St
E 88th St
E 87th St

YORKVILLE

86th St S
E 86th St S
86th St S

E 85th St

Start your evening with a drink at **Ryan's Daughter** (p163).
🚶 7 min from 86th St station

Grab lunch in the 1950s-inspired **Lexington Candy Shop** (p158).
🚶 5 min from 86th St station

Park Ave
Lexington Ave
Third Ave
Second Ave
First Ave
York Ave
East End Ave

East River

E 79th St

77th St S
E 77th St
E 76th St

Down a beer and watch live bands perform at **American Trash** (p163).
🚶 17 min from 72nd St station

AMERICAN Bar

UPPER EAST SIDE

E 75th St
E 74th St

Satisfy your shopping urges at **Ralph Lauren** (p164).
🚶 7 min from 68th St-Hunter College station

E 72nd St
E 71st St

72nd St S

Sample a fleet of craft beers at **Pony Bar** (p163) along with its famous double-fried wings.
🚶 13 min from 72nd St station

Franklin D Roosevelt Dr

0
0
500 m
0.25 miles

29 ART GEMS
on Museum Mile

MUSEUMS | DINING | ARCHITECTURE

The Met and Guggenheim museums draw thousands every year to the Upper East Side. In addition to these institutions there are private art collections and smaller museums dedicated to Renaissance and modern artists. You can even wander through some historic mansions restored as beautiful galleries.

WANGKUN JIA/SHUTTERSTOCK ©

◫ How To

Getting around 6 line to the 86th St station on Lexington. From there, walk toward Fifth Ave and Central Park or take the M86 crosstown bus.

When to go To avoid crowds, visit galleries before 1pm, especially on school weekdays. Check websites for gallery hours.

Stroll in the park The galleries are all within walking distance of Central Park.

Free entry Most galleries are free entry, though with a suggested donation.

VIVIAN CHEN/ALAMY STOCK PHOTO ©

Art in Historic Residences

Once you arrive on the corner of 86th St after walking up from the Lexington Ave train station, you will see an old mansion that is home to the **Neue Galerie**. Inside the refined establishment built in 1914 is a collection of priceless German and Austrian art. The two-floor home has paintings by Dagobert Peche and fine jewelry by Josef Hoffman. The grand jewel of the collection is the painting *Woman in Gold* by Gustav Klimt.

Contemporary Meets Traditional

Closer to the Met is the **Tambaran Gallery** on 82nd St. Come here to see more contemporary artists of African, Asian and Indigenous origins, as the gallery focuses on underrepresented voices in the art world.

OSUGI/SHUTTERSTOCK ©

🏛 Stunning Buildings

Much of the architecture along the Museum Mile is itself a work of art, most notably the **Guggenheim**. The **Jewish Museum**, designed by CPH Gilbert, features Gothic-inspired opulence. The **Cooper Hewitt, Smithsonian Design Museum** is another notable structure, boasting red brick and limestone in addition to Tiffany glass windows.

Above left Neue Galerie
Above right Cooper Hewitt, Smithsonian Design Museum **Left** Jewish Museum

Check out the sculptures too. The next block over is the **Bonner David Galleries**, which has lesser-known contemporary paintings and sculptures by the likes of Gail Morris and Milt Kobayashi. It also has more abstract pieces, plus a small collection of more traditional artists, such as Luis Giatti. The **Sundaram Tagore Gallery**, on Madison Ave near 82nd St, stands out from its peers due to its focus on Eastern art with various global influences, and its unique and vibrant imagery and installations. You'll end your walk at 79th St for the **Skarstedt Gallery**, which features lesser-known works from famous names such as Andy Warhol and KAWS. It's a great spot for art enthusiasts who've already covered the well-known art galleries.

Frick Madison

This beautiful collection includes artworks from the Renaissance through to the 20th century and should not be missed. Admission for adults is $22, with students receiving a discounted admission with proper ID. If you come on Thursday evening, you can pay-as-you-want to get inside between 4pm and 6pm. Inside, visitors will be greeted by a range of sculptures, ceramics and paintings by big names such as Rembrandt, Jean-Honoré Fragonard and JMW Turner. There's also a cafe upstairs at which visitors can grab a quick bite to eat or a coffee before moving on to the next stop on their itinerary.

By Alfred Pommer, *owner, NYC Cultural Walking Tours; tours focused on history and landmarks*

FAR LEFT: DPA PICTURE ALLIANCE/ALAMY STOCK PHOTO © LEFT: DANA GIVENS ©

Left Frick Madison **Below** Sistina

Lunch in Style

The neighborhood has no shortage of exclusive restaurants. For a lavish neighborhood lunch, sample the great wine selection and an assortment of fresh, delicious pasta at **Sistina**. Sit outside in the right season, but note that the interior, with crown moldings and vivid wall art, is worth staying inside for. **Caravaggio** is another luxury Italian lunch option and also a great people-watching spot. Keep in mind that many of these upscale restaurants close between 3pm and 5pm to prepare for the dinner rush.

Travel in Time at Lexington Candy Shop

NEW YORK'S OLDEST FAMILY-RUN LUNCHEONETTE

New York City has no shortage of fine dining, especially concentrated in the exclusive neighborhood of the Upper East Side. Amid this competitive scene, the Lexington Candy Shop stands out from the crowd. As the oldest family-run luncheonette in the city, and the last of its kind, it's become an area landmark.

DANA GIVENS ©

Origin Story

After being opened in 1925 by Soterios Philis and Tami Naskos, the Lexington Candy Shop became a fixture throughout the Great Depression. The famed eatery has worked to preserve its charm through the ages, so much so that present-day patrons feel like they've traveled back through time to enjoy homemade burgers and shakes on an old-school lunch date. It's still run by descendants of the original owner, who have honored their commitment to American homestyle dishes.

Candy Store to Luncheonette

When it first opened, the shop got its name from its delicious homemade candies, which became popular among locals, as did its soda fountain. Chocolates were made in the basement until 1948, when the family decided to discontinue their candy selection and turn the shop into a full-time luncheonette. Its conspicuous corner location helped attract locals and tourists alike.

Today, the luncheonette welcomes a mix of local residents – many of whom make the same order on each visit – and international visitors fresh from nearby museums and looking to step back in time for a vintage dining experience. Like the eatery itself, staff have weathered the changing trends of the frenetic NYC dining scene for decades by staying true to tradition, until eventually the old ways became new again to fresh generations of diners.

Pictured Lexington Candy Shop

Famous Films, Famous Faces

The famous Coca-Cola bottle window sits under neon signage – along with numerous profiles, and photos of the rock stars and famous comedians who have visited over the years. The eatery has its own claims to fame, having been featured in commercials, television and even films such as *Three Days of the Condor*, *Fading Gigolo* and *The Nanny Diaries*.

Menu Full of Tradition

Like the eatery itself, staff have weathered the changing trends of the frenetic NYC dining scene for decades by staying true to tradition.

In accordance with the philosophy of its third-generation owners, the Lexington Candy Shop's menu, methods and ingredients are much as they were back when it first opened its doors in the early 1900s. The juices are still freshly squeezed, the burgers time-proven classics, the recipes untouched. Even the Coca-Cola is made by hand with fresh syrup. The eatery is the only one of its kind left today: serving breakfast, lunch and treats like milkshakes, before closing at 6pm just ahead of the dinner rush. Inside its small corner location are just a couple of intimate booths and a countertop nostalgic for its old-time roots.

🍨 Sweet Satisfaction

The luncheonette may not have any candy anymore, but you can still satisfy your sweet tooth with its famous ice-cream fountains and floats. The milkshakes are made with a 1940s-style blender and served in four classic flavors: vanilla, chocolate, strawberry and coffee. Beside the counter you'll find a small collection of vintage candies like Turkish delight; behind it you'll see some of the mixers and utensils used to make them back in the 1940s. And that's what the Lexington Candy Shop is about: finding a home for the past in the present.

30 An Upper East Side
AFTERNOON

SHOPPING | RESTAURANTS | ART

Iconic television shows like *Gossip Girl* show off the old-money allure of this well-heeled neighborhood. In fact, some visitors tailor small-screen-inspired itineraries that involve walking famous avenues, browsing glamorous shopfronts and swooning over luxury brands, just as their television counterparts do.

FRANCES ROBERTS/ALAMY STOCK PHOTO ©

🗺 Trip Notes

Getting here Take the N/R/Q to 72nd St station, and the crosstown M72 bus to Fifth Ave or Madison Ave.

When to go Start around noon so you have plenty of time before rush hour begins at 4pm.

Dress to impress Dress stylishly as preparation for great photo ops at various shops. You'll also want to blend in with the trendy local fashion you'll encounter on your travels.

📷 Brand-Name Sightseeing

It's possible to live out your Upper East Side luxury fantasy without a millionaire's budget. A walk along Madison Ave will not only let you window-shop luxury brands such as Christian Louboutin, but also take you past sites made recognizable by famous television shows, movies and books.

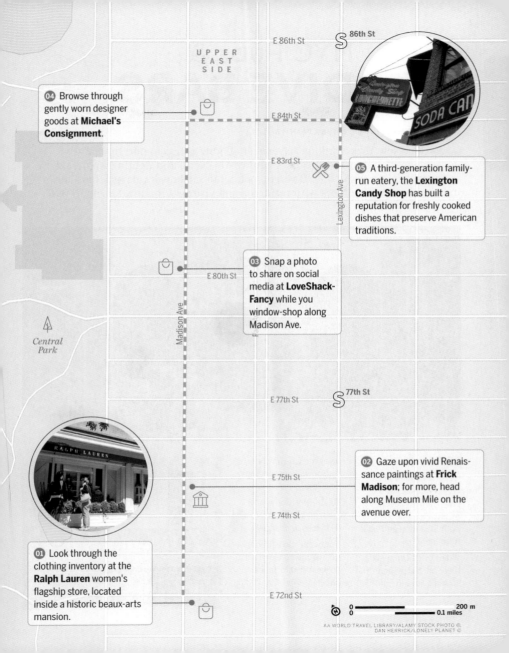

UPPER
EAST
SIDE

E 86th St

S 86th St

04 Browse through gently worn designer goods at **Michael's Consignment**.

E 84th St

E 83rd St

Lexington Ave

05 A third-generation family-run eatery, the **Lexington Candy Shop** has built a reputation for freshly cooked dishes that preserve American traditions.

03 Snap a photo to share on social media at **LoveShack-Fancy** while you window-shop along Madison Ave.

E 80th St

Madison Ave

Central Park

E 77th St

S 77th St

02 Gaze upon vivid Renaissance paintings at **Frick Madison**; for more, head along Museum Mile on the avenue over.

E 75th St

E 74th St

01 Look through the clothing inventory at the **Ralph Lauren** women's flagship store, located inside a historic beaux-arts mansion.

E 72nd St

0   200 m
0   0.1 miles

31

NYC Pubs & DIVE BARS

DRINKS | NIGHTLIFE | ENTERTAINMENT

The New York drinking scene isn't all glitz and glamour. In fact, it's densely populated by no-frills bars with rustic decor, dim lighting, sports on TV, and sometimes a pool table. If you're looking to see how locals kick back, drop into a pub and rub elbows with residents and visitors for a low-key night out.

ROBERT K. CHIN - STOREFRONTS/ALAMY STOCK PHOTO ©

🗺 How To

Getting around Most bars are concentrated past Third and Second Aves. Catch the Q line to 86th St station and walk from there.

When to go On weekdays there are happy-hour specials around 5pm. On weekends, begin your pub crawl between 6pm and 7pm.

Cash rules Come with cash on hand to avoid ATM fees or charges.

Footwear You'll probably be walking between bars, so wear comfortable shoes.

ROBERT K. CHIN - STOREFRONTS/ALAMY STOCK PHOTO ©

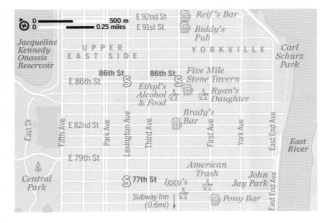

Casual Hangouts

Pubs and dive bars have become staples in the Yorkville area of the Upper East Side, particularly along First and Second Aves. Take the Q train to 86th St, then walk to two popular neighborhood haunts. The first one is **Five Mile Stone Tavern**, which has an outdoor balcony patio and a vintage feel. Check to see what its weekly specials are (they change regularly) and scan the beer menu, which has a nice mixture of imported and domestic choices on tap.

Walk down the street toward First Ave and you'll find **Ryan's Daughter**, another local hangout with a casual atmosphere. Established in 1979, it has since become a neighborhood hangout spot that attracts both locals and visitors.

Head further uptown toward 96th St for more options, including shooting darts under a web of Christmas lights at **Biddy's Pub**, and the relaxed vibe and party-friendly setting of **Brady's Bar**. If it's a nice enough night, walk to **Reif's Bar** on 92nd St and sit outside on its outdoor patio. In the other direction, head to **Pony Bar** and order a fleet of craft beers – it's the best selection in the area and Pony has a livelier atmosphere than most. When you're done with your bar-hopping, and are looking for more entertainment, catch live music at **American Trash**.

Top left Ethyl's Alcohol & Food
Bottom left Subway Inn

Karaoke & Themed Bars

Karaoke nights and daily happy-hour specials from 7pm to 4am mean **Iggy's** stands out as one of the best dive bars not only in the area but in the entire city. **Subway Inn**, which dates back to 1937, is another notorious local hangout and highly rated dive bar where you can still enjoy a cheap beer. Nostalgics should stop by **Ethyl's Alcohol & Food**, a '70s-themed bar, for a cocktail or two and (depending on the schedule) a live show.

Listings

BEST OF THE REST

🛍 Trendy Boutiques

LoveShackFancy

A trendy Madison Ave boutique with floral designs for women. It has an Instagrammable wall on the side street that you can photograph after your shopping excursion. Expect to see mostly dresses and threads for spring and summer.

Alexis Bittar

Always filled with shoppers browsing the safari-themed jewelry. Most of the finds inside will be made from precious metals and Swarovski crystals.

Mixology

Originally from Long Island, the Manhattan outpost is a haven for popular designer names. Mostly fast-fashion brands comparable to H&M or Forever 21.

Yumi Kim

A New York–based womenswear designer with a breezy, relaxed vibe, and with hanging birdcages and peacock wallpaper.

Ralph Lauren

Visit the men's flagship to see the beautiful store located inside the Ralph Lauren mansion. Within walking distance of Central Park.

DIGS

A popular local womenswear shop featuring high-end European brands as well as in-house designs and accessories.

Bonne Nuit

A small store for luxury baby's and children's wear from high-end European designers. Visitors can also find luxury loungewear and pajamas for women.

☕ Cafes & Bakeries

Levian Bakery $$

A small bakery known for its incredibly tasty cookies and ice-cream sandwiches, which come in flavors such as chocolate-chip walnut or dark-chocolate peanut butter.

Stella & Fly $$

Coffee cafe meets wine bar. Stop by for an afternoon or evening outing. Or try the happy hour between noon and 8pm weekdays. Check the website for live shows.

Orwashers Bakery $$

Founded by a Hungarian family in 1916, this bakery is known for its freshly baked breads, doughnuts, chocolates and bagels.

Ralph Lauren shirts

By the Way Bakery $$

An old-school eatery that prides itself on crafting classic American treats, from an assortment of cookies to specialty cakes.

Padoca Bakery $$

Known for its Brazilian cheese breads, this is a great spot to grab a coffee and sample a freshly baked pastry.

Sweet Shop NYC $$

A retro-style dessert shop offering gourmet ice creams and gelatos. Also has hard-to-find candies.

Lunch & Wine Menu

Penrose $$

A premium bar with wooden decor and old-fashioned cocktails. It stays open until 2am, but it's best for lunch or a weekend brunch. Extensive wine and spirits menu.

Libertador $$

This Argentinian restaurant boasts great food and a long list of regional wines served with a nice cut of steak. Hearty portions. Always ask what the weekly specials are.

Uva $$

Enjoy a late lunch with home-style Italian fare in this cozy, intimate restaurant with an impressive wine list. It has a late-night menu until 2am – perfect for those looking for post-party meals.

Kaia $$

An intimate bar with a menu focused on South African wines. Offers small plates such as fresh oysters and duck wings. One of the more unique restaurants in the area.

Orwashers Bakery

Serena's Wine Bar $$

A cozy bar boasting a lengthy wine menu with salads and small serving plates spotlighting Italian cuisine, like beef meatballs.

Vintage Shopping

Encore

A walk-up consignment store on 84th St where shoppers can browse and find vintage designer threads costing between $300 and $700.

Michael's Consignment

Searching for the perfect pair of Manolos or luxury silk scarves? Michael's is a great apartment-style shop with designer items.

La Boutique Resale

Browse though the top names in fashion, from Fendi to Moschino and Etro. Comb through the aisles to find some reasonably priced items.

 Scan to find more things to do on the Upper East Side online

HARLEM

RESTAURANTS | HISTORY | ARTS

Dr Martin Luther King Jr Boulevard

W 125 St

Experience
Harlem
online

HARLEM
Trip Builder

**TAKE YOUR PICK OF MUST-SEES
AND HIDDEN GEMS**

■■■■ Harlem is known for its vibrancy and historic African American roots. It's that unique cultural identity that has defined its character. Expect a more laid-back atmosphere, as the area is still mostly residential with not too many hotel options. From its storied restaurants to its music venues, you can expect to have a good time with a lot of entertainment when visiting Harlem.

🏙 Neighborhood Notes

Best for Happy hours, good music, affordable prices.

Transport 2/3 trains travel along Lenox Ave. Take the crosstown bus at 116th St station to reach East Harlem.

Getting around Walking is best. Stick to Lenox Ave for most attractions and restaurants.

Tip Most establishments close between 7pm and 8pm.

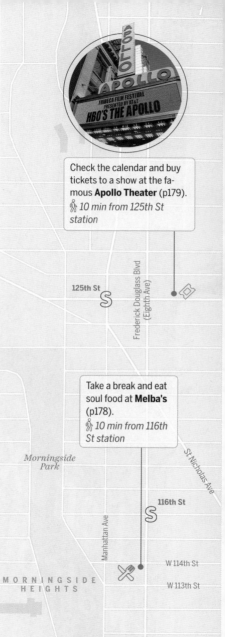

Check the calendar and buy tickets to a show at the famous **Apollo Theater** (p179).
🚶 *10 min from 125th St station*

125th St

Frederick Douglass Blvd
(Eighth Ave)

Take a break and eat soul food at **Melba's** (p178).
🚶 *10 min from 116th St station*

Morningside Park

St Nicholas Ave

116th St

Manhattan Ave

W 114th St

MORNINGSIDE HEIGHTS

W 113th St

Browse through the archives at the **Schomburg Center of Black Research** (p173).
🚶 1 min from 135th St station

Dance to African and Caribbean tunes along with live music at the **Shrine** (p179) with cocktails.
🚶 7 min from 135th St station

Enjoy a live music show with dinner at **Ginny's Supper Club** (p179) below the Red Rooster.
🚶 3 min from 125th St station

Taste authentic Puerto Rican cuisine at **Cuchifritos** (p171).
🚶 3 min from 116th St station

Sample Senegalese and Somali food in **Little Africa** (p174)
🚶 1 min from 116th St station

Stroll through **La Marqueta** (p171) market for traditional Caribbean and Latin foods.
🚶 6 min from 110th St station or 116th St station

W 135th St
135th St
E 135th St

W 134th St
W 133rd St

Adam Clayton Powell Jr Blvd (Seventh Ave)

Malcolm X Blvd (Lenox Ave)

Fifth Ave

Madison Ave

Harlem River

W 128th St

HARLEM

Martin Luther King Jr Blvd (W 125th St)
125th St

Marcus Garvey Park

Third Ave

Second Ave

116th St
W 116th St

116th St
E 116th St (Luis Munoz Marin Blvd)

SPANISH HARLEM

E 115th St

Park Ave

Lexington Ave

E 112th St

0
0
500 m
0.25 miles

32

A Taste of
EL BARRIO

MARKETS | RESTAURANTS | CULTURE

▬▬▬ Spanish Harlem, also known as El Barrio, is home to a mixture of cultures. This diversity is reflected in the local markets and the rich and varied cuisine, which you can sample on a walk around the neighborhood, trying foods with Mexican, Puerto Rican and Dominican roots as you go.

RICHARD LEVINE/ALAMY STOCK PHOTO ©

🚚 Latin Foods on the Go

East Harlem has become home to a vibrant community of Latin immigrants primarily of Puerto Rican, Mexican and Dominican descent, and nearby restaurants showcase that diversity in their food. The Puerto Rican community has particularly deep roots here, and its cuisine is prevalent. Snacks like empanadas and *pastelitos* are popular and common.

🗺 Trip Notes

Getting here Take the 6 train to 116th St station and walk down. It's a small, concentrated area, so it's very walkable.

When to go Start around noon or go for happy hour and an early dinner.

Language At smaller eateries many of the workers speak mostly Spanish with little English.

Cash rules Street vendors are plentiful, so have cash on hand.

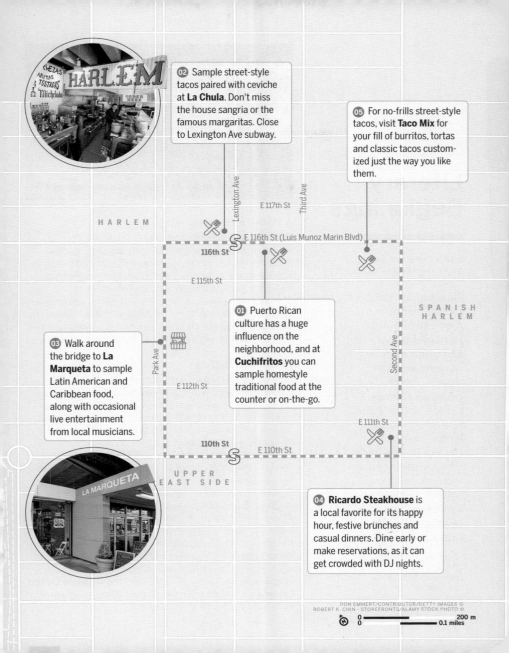

02 Sample street-style tacos paired with ceviche at **La Chula**. Don't miss the house sangria or the famous margaritas. Close to Lexington Ave subway.

05 For no-frills street-style tacos, visit **Taco Mix** for your fill of burritos, tortas and classic tacos customized just the way you like them.

01 Puerto Rican culture has a huge influence on the neighborhood, and at **Cuchifritos** you can sample homestyle traditional food at the counter or on-the-go.

03 Walk around the bridge to **La Marqueta** to sample Latin American and Caribbean food, along with occasional live entertainment from local musicians.

04 **Ricardo Steakhouse** is a local favorite for its happy hour, festive brunches and casual dinners. Dine early or make reservations, as it can get crowded with DJ nights.

HARLEM

SPANISH HARLEM

UPPER EAST SIDE

Lexington Ave
Third Ave
Park Ave
Second Ave

E 117th St
E 116th St (Luis Munoz Marin Blvd)
116th St
E 115th St
E 112th St
E 111th St
110th St
E 110th St

0   200 m
0   0.1 miles

RAYMOND BOYD/MICHAEL OCHS ARCHIVES/GETTY IMAGES ©

Literary Beginnings

THE SEEDS OF THE HARLEM RENAISSANCE

Famous for its historic roots in African American culture, Harlem was home to and inspiration for numerous prolific writers, such as Langston Hughes, Claude McKay, Ralph Ellison and Richard Wright, during the Harlem Renaissance. Today, visitors can see where these famous writers resided and wrote some of their most acclaimed works.

Left Langston Hughes House, Harlem **Middle** Harlem YMCA **Right** Schomburg Center of Black Research

A Walk in Harlem

The arts are woven into the history of Harlem. Prolific writers such as Richard Wright and Langston Hughes have contributed to the neighborhood's storied history of African American artists. The Harlem Renaissance, which lasted throughout the roaring twenties, was a period of immense creativity among the artists who had been attracted to the neighborhood. Many of those figures have become the foundation of African American literature and have inspired some of the greatest contemporary writers.

Langston Hughes

Poet Langston Hughes, who arrived in the 1920s after briefly attending Columbia University, emerged as one of the stars of the Harlem Renaissance. In his autobiography, *The Big Sea* (1940), Hughes talks at length about his love for the neighborhood and its thriving arts scene. He stayed in the community, living in brownstone where he wrote most of his famous works until he died in 1967. The home still stands, not far from the Apollo Theater and Sylvia's Restaurant.

In his biography Hughes describes how many of the neighborhood's artists would convene at the home of A'Lelia Walker, daughter of Madame CJ Walker. The latter was a well-known socialite who often hosted soirees for the Black arts and social scene. Writer and painter Richard Bruce Nugent and muralist and illustrator Aaron Douglas were among those who could be found at Walker's famous parties. Today, the building is the **Countee Cullen Library**, named after the famed poet (*Color;* 1925) and novelist of the Harlem Renaissance.

Famous Writer Haunts

Many famous haunts frequented by influential writers are still standing. For example, the **Harlem YMCA** building once domiciled famous writers Richard Wright (*Native Son;* 1940. *Black Boy;* 1945), Ralph Ellison (*Invisible Man;* 1952) and Claude McKay (*Home to Harlem;* 1928), and across the street is the **James Weldon Johnson Residence Apartments**, where the late leader of the National Association for the Advancement of Colored People (NAACP) resided between 1925 and 1938, during which time he published various works of poetry and social studies

> The Harlem Renaissance, which lasted throughout the twenties, was a period of immense creativity among the artists who had been attracted to the neighborhood.

Visible History

In Harlem, there is much history standing in plain sight, telling the stories of the notable people that lived them and helped craft the culture that still endures today. On just a brief walk of the neighborhood's busy center, visitors can learn about its rich history in the arts and its impact on the locals and transplants who have made it home.

ⓘ Schomburg Center

For those who want to know more about historic Harlem, the Schomburg Center of Black Research houses archives containing literary works and souvenirs of notable Black artists and other figures who helped shape Harlem and impacted African American culture. Before it was a library, the center – named after Afro–Puerto Rican writer, historian and activist Arturo Schomburg – was home of the WPA's Federal Writers' Project during the Great Depression, before becoming a theater that hosted the debuts of Sidney Poitier and Harry Belafonte.

33 Little Africa's
FEASTS

FOOD | RESTAURANTS | CULTURE

Little Africa is at the heart of Harlem's diverse interaction between West and East African cultures. From its small shops and local market to its restaurants and their vibrant presentation of the continent's varied cuisines, you won't find anything else like it in the city.

VESPASIAN/ALAMY STOCK PHOTO ©

How To

Getting here 2/3 train to the 116th St station. From there walk west across the different avenues.

When to go Many small restaurants have great lunch specials, and the crowds will be small.

Cash rules If shopping at small shops or local markets, bring cash.

Central location Several subway lines service this area, making downtown trips easy.

RICHARD LEVINE/ALAMY STOCK PHOTO ©

LOTTIE DAVIES/LONELY PLANET ©

Open-Air Market

Next to the MIST Harlem restaurant, the **Malcolm Shabazz Harlem Market** is an open-air affair with merchants from various African countries. The market sells an assortment of different products such as handbags, unique sculptures for the home, and skincare products ranging from African black soap to shea butter, which are wonderful for the skin and budget-friendly. This is the ideal place to grab a souvenir of your trip to Little Africa. The quality of the imported goods sold means many of the items are better than equivalents sold in stores. There are also stalls selling garments made with African fabric where shoppers can get purchases tailored. The market is open year-round.

West Africa in Upper Manhattan

In a small stretch of city blocks is a concentration of African immigrants, particularly from western Africa, who have carved out a section of the neighborhood for shops. These shops cater to cultural needs, ranging from imported goods that can't be found in regular stores to restaurants serving traditional meals.

Above left and left Malcolm Shabazz Harlem Market **Above right** Flags of African nations, African American Day Parade,

Food of the African Diaspora

Continue west and you'll come across other small African-owned shops and restaurants intermingled with locally owned boutiques and convenience stores. For lunch, stop in at one of the many African restaurants in the area, such as Senegalese cuisine at **Keur Coumba** or **Pikine**, where you can enjoy savory stews made with cassava and other fresh ingredients. Top off this vibrant

introduction to a different cultural palate with *bissap* or ginger juice. Another popular eatery is the **Safari**, where foodies can sample Somalian dishes like *hilib ari*, which is roasted goat served on Somali basmati rice; or a *sabaayed* wrap with homemade *chappati* bread. It doesn't offer African cuisine, but for dessert stop for freshly made sweet or savory crepes at the **Crepe Bakery**.

✗ Le Pétit Senegal

Little Africa is also known as Le Pétit Senegal for the large population of Senegalese residents living there, which is why visitors may find so many restaurants focused on the country's cuisine and overhear conversation in French. Today, the locals represent numerous West African countries, including Guinea, Burkina Faso and Ghana. You can also venture outside Little Africa to visit other Harlem-based African eateries, such as **Accra** on 125th St and the **Ponty Bistro** further up on 139th St.

By Linda Adria Moscovitz, *private chef who specializes in African food tours and pop-up eateries in Harlem,* @lindaacooks

Left Senegalese women, Harlem
Below Amy Ruth's

Historic Harlem

Mixed in with its African-owned establishments, Little Africa has other notable eateries, such as **Amy Ruth's**. This famous restaurant has been a neighborhood institution for decades and is known for traditional Southern-style comfort food, such as its notorious chicken and waffles. It's normal to see a crowd on Sundays, especially after church services.

Listings

BEST OF THE REST

🍴 Dine-In Restaurants

Vinateria $$

A Spanish- and Italian-influenced eatery that is great for a casual dinner date. The scallop appetizer is savory and delicious! It's a perfect spot for wine-lovers with a great happy hour and wine list to pair with your food.

Melba's $$

Iconic soul-food restaurant. Lunches tend to be relaxed and dinners hectic. The oxtails, collard greens and mac 'n' cheese are a few of the menu favorites. Expect to hear festive music and witness dancing to jazz.

Abyssinia $$

One of the best spots in the city for traditional Ethiopian cuisine. Usually very slow during the day. The hearty portions make it a great place to come for big-group dining.

Babbalucci $$

Authentic Italian fare in the heart of Harlem. The pizza is made in a traditional brick oven and it's amazing. Sit outside on a nice night for happy-hour specials.

Seasoned Vegan $$

Excellent option for those who have a plant-based diet or are interested in sampling vegan food. Menu includes vegan takes on soul-food classics such as BBQ riblets, po'boy sandwiches and a version of Harlem's famous chopped cheeseburger.

Lolo's Seafood Shack $$

Lolo's is known for its crab legs, so don't leave without getting a little dirty cracking some shells. Have a glass of its signature Lolo's Punch made with sorrel and Caribbean rum.

Maison Harlem $$

This classic French bistro in the middle of West Harlem is a great dinner-date option and boasts an extensive wine menu.

🍺 Beer & Cocktails

Harlem Hops $$

A low-key brewery with great music and selection of locally brewed beers on tap. There's a small patio in the back if inside is too loud for you. The menu changes periodically.

Corner Social $$

A popular spot for late-night parties, boozy brunches and all-around good time. The drinks are strong and reasonably priced. Be sure to try the house sangria and the Harlem Love Punch.

67 Orange $$

For those that fancy artisanal and upscale drinks, 67 Orange is a chill speakeasy-type bar. It's an ideal spot to rest and drink one of the signature cocktails, such as the Santa Rockey.

Harlem Tavern $$

A chill and casual beer garden that gets pretty loud and packed on weekends. The food

Melba's

menu is extensive – try the tavern-style mac 'n' cheese. Ask the server what the brew of the month is.

Cantina Taqueria & Tequila Bar $$

A great place for cheap eats and strong drinks. The margaritas are super and the tacos perfectly sized. Another local happy-hour favorite that fills pretty quickly.

♫ Live Music

Shrine

Chill bar that hosts live bands and local artists. Stay after midnight for the DJ parties, featuring R&B, reggae, salsa and traditional African music.

Ginny's Supper Club

Directly under Red Rooster, the lively supper club hosts live band performances. Separate menu from its sister restaurant upstairs.

Minton's Playhouse

Come enjoy dinner and a fancy cocktail to a live jazz band. Check the calendar online to see what the weekly lineup looks like.

Apollo Theater

Legendary venue where major artists have been discovered. This landmark theater still hosts concerts and events.

✖ Brunch Weekends

Angel of Harlem $$

A lively eatery that hosts popular brunches with great music and vibes. Serves Caribbean-inspired dishes.

Maxwell's Central Park $$

A rustic eatery right next to Central Park. The bottomless brunch brings in a large crowd every weekend, and the signature cocktails are some of the best around. Ask the bartender for the seasonal specials.

Harlem Tavern

Amy Ruth's $$

A famous eatery that lives up to its name. Please treat yourself to the chicken or catfish with waffles. The brunch is still a neighborhood favorite every Sunday, especially after church service.

Lido Harlem Restaurant $$

Another bottomless brunch that is ranked one of the best in Harlem, and for good reason. Enjoy unlimited mimosas with freshly baked crepes and other authentic Italian fare.

B Squared Harlem $$$

A speakeasy-type establishment with a tasty brunch menu, including shrimp and grits, and lobster hash, along with matcha coconut pancakes. The drink to try is the Mama We Outside to kick off the festivities.

Edge $$

This Caribbean restaurant is known for becoming a party during weekend brunches. The menu blends the best of Jamaican and American cuisine such as jerk chicken with fluffy waffles.

Scan to find more things to do in Harlem online

QUEENS

MUSEUMS | RESTAURANTS | CULTURE

Experience Queens online

QUEENS
Trip Builder

**TAKE YOUR PICK OF MUST-SEES
AND HIDDEN GEMS**

▬▬▬ While New York City is known for being a melting pot, the borough of Queens is at the center of what makes the city a cultural mosaic. From its famous night markets in Flushing's Chinatown to its collection of art museums in Long Island City, Queens has a lot to offer when it comes to creating immersive cultural experiences in its different neighborhoods.

🗺️ Neighborhood Notes

Best for Restaurants and arts-focused galleries with an occasional museum visit.

Transport The 7, M, N/R and W trains serve most attractions. The A train takes you to Far Rockaway.

Getting around Travel to distant destinations like Flushing on weekdays to avoid subway interruptions and delays.

Tip Travel times can be lengthy, so make it a day trip.

Take an art walk in **Socrates Sculpture Park** (p189) with its gorgeous views of the Manhattan skyline.
🚶 20 min from Broadway station

See contemporary art and visit the galleries at **MoMA PS1** (p189) which also hosts DJ parties.
🚶 13 min from Court Sq station

Hell Gate
Astoria Park
Main Ave
Roosevelt Island
Astoria Blvd
ASTORIA
East River
Vernon Blvd
Broadway
34th Ave
21st St
Steinway St
31st St
LONG ISLAND CITY
39th St
Jackson Ave
SUNNYSIDE
Queens Blvd
48th St
Greenpoint Ave
Grand St
BUSHWICK

MoMA PS1

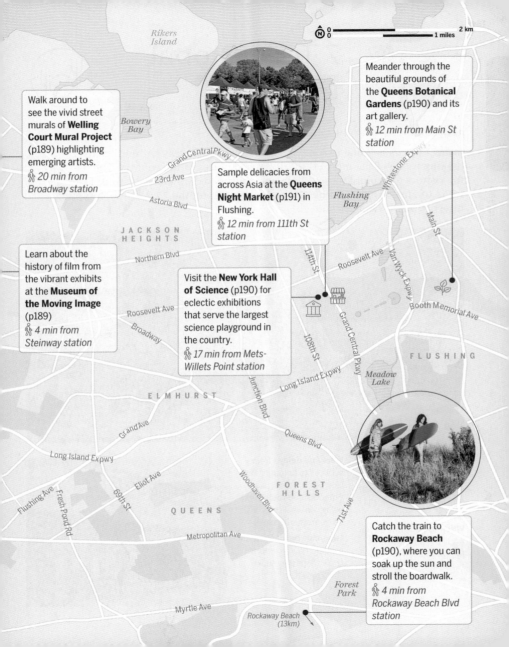

Walk around to see the vivid street murals of **Welling Court Mural Project** (p189) highlighting emerging artists.
🚶 20 min from Broadway station

Meander through the beautiful grounds of the **Queens Botanical Gardens** (p190) and its art gallery.
🚶 12 min from Main St station

Sample delicacies from across Asia at the **Queens Night Market** (p191) in Flushing.
🚶 12 min from 111th St station

Learn about the history of film from the vibrant exhibits at the **Museum of the Moving Image** (p189)
🚶 4 min from Steinway station

Visit the **New York Hall of Science** (p190) for eclectic exhibitions that serve the largest science playground in the country.
🚶 17 min from Mets-Willets Point station

Catch the train to **Rockaway Beach** (p190), where you can soak up the sun and stroll the boardwalk.
🚶 4 min from Rockaway Beach Blvd station

Rikers Island

Bowery Bay

Grand Central Pkwy

23rd Ave

Astoria Blvd

JACKSON HEIGHTS

Northern Blvd

Roosevelt Ave

Broadway

ELMHURST

Grand Ave

Long Island Expwy

Flushing Ave

Fresh Pond Rd

69th St

Eliot Ave

QUEENS

Metropolitan Ave

Myrtle Ave

Junction Blvd

Woodhaven Blvd

FOREST HILLS

71st Ave

Forest Park

Rockaway Beach (13km)

Flushing Bay

Whitestone Expwy

Main St

Roosevelt Ave

Van Wyck Expwy

Booth Memorial Ave

FLUSHING

114th St

108th St

Grand Central Pkwy

Long Island Expwy

Meadow Lake

Queens Blvd

0 2 km
0 1 miles
N

34 7 Train Global **FEAST**

RESTAURANTS | CULTURE | SHOPPING

■■■■ Queens is home to some of the most diverse areas within the city, making it one of the most ethnically varied places in the country. The best way for visitors to explore these ethnic neighborhoods, which range from Little India to Flushing's Chinatown, is to hop on and off the 7 train line, sampling international cuisine as you go.

SNAPASKYLINE/SHUTTERSTOCK ©

🗺 How To

Getting here From Manhattan catch the 7 train at 42nd St-Bryant Park and 34th St-Hudson Yards.

When to go This is easily a day trip so start early to give yourself time between different stops.

Weekend delays Train services to boroughs outside Manhattan typically experience re-routes and delays on weekends. Visit on weekdays for ease.

Language barrier In some neighborhoods clerks at small shops may speak little English.

IRA BERGER/ALAMY STOCK PHOTO ©

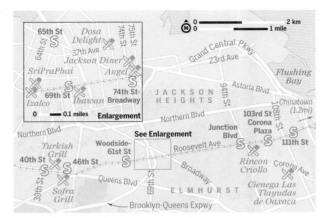

Top left Flushing Chinatown
Bottom left Jackson Diner

Diverse Palate

Between the train stops at 40th and Lowery St is Sunnyside. Although a multicultural community, Sunnyside is specifically known as a hub for quality Turkish restaurants such as the **Turkish Grill**, which is close to the train station, or the **Sofra Grill**, which serves laid-back Mediterranean food.

At Woodside, you can travel to Little Manila to taste appetizers at the area's string of Filipino restaurants such as dine-in eatery **Ihawan** for savory BBQ in a no-frills setting. It's also a great destination for some of the best Thai restaurants in the city with restaurants like **SriPraPhai**. Between the Woodside and 61st stops, you will also run into Central American restaurants such as El Salvadoran **Izalco**, which offers signature *pupusas* in a cozy ambience and is known for its local crowd. Don't forget to try the horchata with deep-fried plantains.

The next stop on your journey is at 74th St-Broadway station bordering Jackson Heights. This is where you'll find Little India. It's home to shops that specialize in South Asian imports, and to a host of Indian restaurants whose homestyle cooking represents the subcontinent's diverse regional cuisine, such as **Angel** for North Indian street food or **Dosa Delight** for South Indian–style food. **Jackson Diner** has a blend of both and nicely sized portions. Further along the train line, you reach the Corona neighborhood between Junction Blvd and Corona Plaza. Here you can find a variety of Latin American restaurants, ranging from Cuban food at **Rincon Criollo** to Mexican food (try the street tacos) at **Cienega Las Tlayudas de Oaxaca**.

Flushing Chinatown

Saving the best for last is the final stop on the 7 train: Flushing's Chinatown. Come here for a diverse selection of novelty shops and restaurants. Unlike Manhattan's Chinatown, the Flushing edition isn't as tourist driven and is known for being home to some of the best Chinese restaurants in the city. Local favorites include **White Bear** for its amazing dumplings, **Haidilao** for traditional hotpot – particularly well suited to groups looking for large portions and sharable plates (with a massage or manicure while you wait for your table) – and **Szechwan Absolute** for the best Sichuan cuisine in the city. For dessert, go to the **Tai Pan** bakery for Chinese sweets, such as homemade bread or buns.

ART
in Queens

01 Isamu Noguchi

An iconic Japanese artist who was among the 20th century's most prolific sculptors, with a career beginning in the 1920s and spanning several decades. He designed the Noguchi Museum in Long Island City himself.

02 Socrates Sculpture Park

A community park with revolving exhibitions from various artists. It's also the perfect place for a photo op featuring a Manhattan skyline backdrop.

03 Flux Factory

A community space that's a haven for the local Queens art community and its emerging artists.

04 Astoria Performing Arts Center

An arts center known for its small runs of famous productions, with a priority on showcasing local, undiscovered talent.

05 Welling Court Mural Project

A community initiative to beautify the neighborhood with street murals from early and emerging graffiti artists.

06 Jim Henson

Visit the permanent Jim Henson exhibition at the Museum of the Moving Image. It explores the legacy of Henson, creator of *Sesame Street* and *The Muppet Show*.

07 MoMA PS1

This unique outpost of its mother institution in Manhattan focuses on only the most thought-provoking contemporary pieces.

35 **VIBRANT ARTS**
in Long Island City

ART GALLERIES | MUSEUMS | PARKS

Manhattan and Brooklyn aren't the only places where you can visit contemporary-art galleries and walk past vibrant murals. Long Island City is also home to a thriving arts hub where visitors can take a day trip outside the city to visit unique museums and hidden art spaces dedicated to showcasing local talent.

🗺 How To

Getting here Reach Long Island City via the 7 train to Vernon Blvd-Jackson Ave station, then walk or take an Uber or Lyft.

When to go Visit during the day since there are outdoor exhibits. Be mindful of subway interruptions on weekends.

Footwear You'll be doing a lot of walking, so wear comfortable shoes.

Free shuttle In summer take advantage of the LIC Art Bus shuttle, which stops at places such as the Noguchi Museum and MoMA PS1.

Top left Noguchi Museum
Bottom left MoMA PS1

Hidden Arts District

Queens is home to a series of art museums that are worth the journey from Manhattan. The **Socrates Sculpture Park** is unique because it is the only one in the city dedicated to creating and exhibiting large-scale work, and it offers views of the Manhattan skyline from the waterfront. Nearby, and also on Vernon Blvd, is the **Noguchi Museum**, featuring works by Japanese artist Isamu Noguchi, one of the most important sculptors in the 20th century. Learn the artistic process of film at the **Museum of the Moving Image**, home to one of the best film archives in the world. Visitors can learn about the art of filmmaking and its pop-culture legacy. For experimental exhibitions, don't miss **MoMA PS1**. It opened in 1971 and is among the oldest centers for contemporary art in the country.

Private Galleries

Private galleries are also rich sources of contemporary artwork, with galleries like **Flux Factory** promoting emerging artists and their works. The **Fisher Landau Center for Art** is housed in a 25,000-sq-ft former parachute-harness factory, where it showcases well-known artists like Kiki Smith, Jasper Johns and Sherrie Levine.

History in Street Art

After the controversial 2013 whitewashing of the historic mural-covered 5 Pointz factory building in Long Island City, community activists have worked to create safe spaces for graffiti artists to showcase their notable art form, which has deep roots in the area. **Welling Court Mural Project** in Astoria is famous for its vivid murals by local artists, and for its determination to beautify the community and to preserve and promote street art as a valid form of artistic expression.

Listings

BEST OF THE REST

🏞 Parks & Outdoors

Fort Trotten

At the head of Little Neck Bay by the Long Island Sound is a peaceful park that was once a former US Army installation. You can also tour the preserved fortress, which dates back to the Civil War.

Corona Park

Also known as Flushing Meadows, this large park is nice for strolls in good weather. Be sure to check out the different sculptures and works of public art on display.

Kingsland Homestead

Home to the Queens Historical Society and known as a city landmark. Visitors can explore the grounds of the 18th-century home to learn about the history of the area.

Gantry Plaza State Park

Located in Long Island City, where you can see some of the best views of Midtown from the waterside.

Alley Pond Park

A park with a lake by Bayside. Visitors can sign up for the adventure course to go zip-lining, climbing and more.

Astoria Park

Situated by the East River, Astoria Park is a great spot to catch the sunset while picnicking on the grass, and serves as a great photo op.

Queens Botanical Gardens

A vibrant garden spread across 39 acres with an art gallery and arboretum in Flushing.

Rockaway Beach

Local sandy beach for swimming and sunbathing with a 5.5-mile boardwalk and seasonal vendors.

🏛 Museums

Queens Museum

A cool, contemporary-art museum in the pavilion that hosted the 1938 World's Fair and serves as an educational center for the local community.

Voelker Orth Museum

Once the home of German immigrants in the late 1800s. Today visitors can walk through the bird sanctuary and the Victorian garden. It's free, with a suggested donation.

New York Hall of Science

The city's only hands-on science center with interactive exhibits and a 3D theater for special presentations.

Sculpture Center

A not-for-profit contemporary-art museum located in Long Island City that dates back to 1928 to support emerging sculptors.

Queens Museum

King Manor Museum

Former home of a New York state senator and signatory of the US Constitution. Now a museum devoted to early life in the local area.

✂ Brunch Hotspots

Sanfords Astoria $$

Right off the Broadway train station is this popular eatery that attracts a crowd for weekend brunches. Expect Mexican-inspired items and a more upscale ambience.

Mom's Kitchen and Bar $$

Start your brunch party at any time of the day at this neighborhood bistro serving classic American fare such as milkshakes and hamburgers.

Shady Lady $$

A popular weekend brunch hangout known for its comfort-food options and tapas menu, making it ideal for bigger groups.

Sugar Freak $$

A Creole restaurant in Astoria offering vibrant brunches and New Orleans–style menu options, such as po'boys and novelty cocktails. Try to get here before 2pm, when the crowd settles in.

No. 5 $$

Weekend vegan brunch specials with non-vegan options plus organic and grass-fed fare and a full bar to satisfy your whole group.

Queens Bully $$

Roomy hangout that specializes in global flavors and BBQ, with strong cocktails.

Queens Center

🏪 Food Courts & Shopping

Queens Center

A huge shopping mall with lots of major brands and chain restaurants.

Queens Crossing

Another popular mall known for shops carrying Asian goods and its large food court. Includes a karaoke lounge.

New World Mall

Inside Flushing's Chinatown, this mall has tons of stores specializing in Asian delicacies and goods. The best part is the food court and its assortment of options.

Queens Night Market

Famous seasonal open-air marketplace to shop for street food from various vendors and see live entertainment.

Scan to find more things to do in Queens online

DAY TRIPS

RECREATION | CULTURE | NATURE

DAY TRIPS
Trip Builder

**TAKE YOUR PICK OF MUST-SEES
AND HIDDEN GEMS**

▬▬▬ One of NYC's greatest attributes is its proximity to destinations that feel worlds apart. Rugged mountains are but an hour away, and buzzy beaches are practically next door. When the city that doesn't sleep leaves you in need of a recharge, these idyllic excursions make for energizing escapes.

🗺 Day Trip Notes

Best for Unique cultural enclaves, lively beaches and sweeping mountain landscapes.

Getting around Public transportation – including Metro North and NJ Transit – makes getting out of the city easy and affordable. Car rentals are notoriously expensive, but they can be beneficial for getting off the beaten path.

Tip Plan ahead for summer trips, particularly in July and August. Type-A New Yorkers are notorious for booking up the best hotels, restaurants and excursions months in advance.

Newburgh ●

Mountainville ○

NEW YORK

Marvel at massive outdoor sculptures at **Storm King** (p204). 🚌 🚆 *2½ hr by train and shuttle*

NEW JERSEY

New York ●

Get a thrill on **Coney Island** (p200) at its seaside amusement parks. 🚆 *1 hr from Midtown*

Long Branch ●

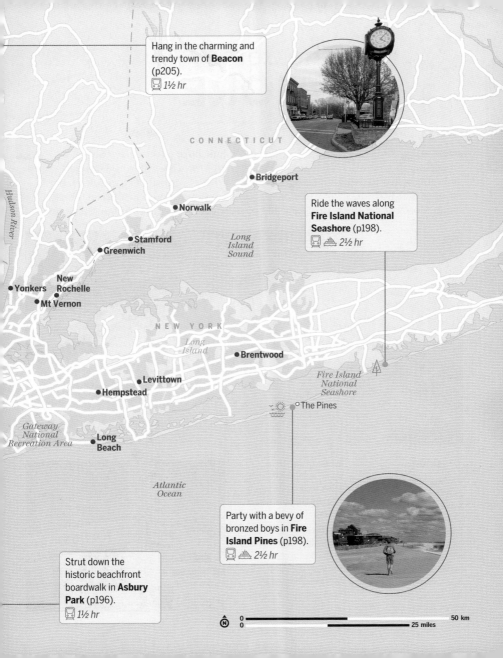

Hang in the charming and trendy town of **Beacon** (p205).
🚆 1½ hr

CONNECTICUT

●Bridgeport

●Norwalk

●Stamford
●Greenwich

Ride the waves along **Fire Island National Seashore** (p198).
🚆 ⛴ 2½ hr

Long Island Sound

Hudson River

New Rochelle
●Yonkers
●Mt Vernon

NEW YORK

Long Island

●Brentwood

●Levittown
●Hempstead

Fire Island National Seashore

🌅 ○ The Pines

Gateway National Recreation Area

●**Long Beach**

Atlantic Ocean

Party with a bevy of bronzed boys in **Fire Island Pines** (p198).
🚆 ⛴ 2½ hr

Strut down the historic beachfront boardwalk in **Asbury Park** (p196).
🚆 1½ hr

0 ——— 50 km
0 ——— 25 miles
Ⓝ

36 The Jersey
SHORE

LIVELY | QUIRKY | HISTORIC

▬▬▬ Artsy and edgy Asbury Park is the Williamsburg of the Jersey Shore: a once-derelict haunt amid a bohemian rebirth. New-wave eateries, boutique shopping and a thriving music scene attract a diverse crowd of city slickers, big families and LGBTIQ+ folks to what's recently become a postcard-perfect hipster hang. Mosey along the historic seaside boardwalk at the center of the renaissance.

SKY CINEMA/SHUTTERSTOCK ©

🗺 How To

Getting here NJ Transit provides direct train service from Penn Station to Asbury Park. The Seastreak Ferry is a scenic but more expensive alternative that docks in Highlands, located 30 minutes north by cab. Budget 90 to 120 minutes if driving.

When to go This is a highly trafficked summer town. Visit in late spring or early autumn to beat the crowds.

Top tip Purchase mandatory beach passes at the beach office or on the Viply app. Cost is $6 for weekdays and $9 for weekends and holidays.

JAMES KIRKIKIS/SHUTTERSTOCK ©

Map labels:
- Sunset Park
- 5th Ave
- 4th Ave
- 3rd Ave
- 2nd Ave
- 1st Ave
- Memorial Dr
- Grand Ave
- ASBURY PARK
- Sunset Ave
- Sunset Lake
- Atlantic Square
- Sunset Pavilion
- Convention Hall & Paramount Theatre
- Playa Bowls
- Ocean Ave
- Silverball Museum Arcade
- Pop's Garage
- Boardwalk
- Asbury Ave
- Main St
- Bond St
- Emory St
- Bangs Ave
- Playa Bowls
- Mogo
- Cookman Ave
- Springwood Ave
- Lake Ave
- Carousel
- Steam Plant
- Atlantic Ocean
- N 0   500 m / 0   0.25 miles

Top left Beach, Asbury Park
Bottom left Wonder Bar

Time travel Imagine Gatsby-era glam while strolling along the seashore. Start by passing through the combined **Convention Hall** and **Paramount Theater**, built between 1928 and 1930 by the same architects behind NYC's Grand Central Terminal. Retired pinball wizards can rediscover their youth at the **Silverball Museum** – a retro arcade with games dating back to the 1930s. To the south, a gutted beaux-arts casino and carousel stand as ghostly reminders of the town's Jazz Age heyday.

Dining and drinks Asbury Park's mile-long boardwalk is an epicurean delight packed with dozens of creative food stalls. Try Korean-fusion tacos at **Mogo**, grab an ear of charred street corn from **Pop's Garage**, or cool down with a fruit smoothie from **Playa Bowls**. Chug rum bowls at **Beach Bar**, mere steps from the sand, or sit on the **Watermark**'s sizable seaside deck for a classy moonlit cocktail hour.

Rock out Music reigns supreme in this Jersey Shore gem, and Bruce Springsteen is the scene's favorite son. Follow his path to fame by heading to the **Stone Pony**, a boardwalk-adjacent rock club where he got his start in the 1970s. Check the venue's Summer Stage schedule to see big-name acts perform under the stars. Up-and-coming talents bring rock, funk, pop and punk to spots like the **Asbury Park Yacht Club** and **Wonder Bar**.

Seaside Street Art

The Wooden Walls Project beautifies Asbury Park's boardwalk with murals created by prominent street artists. See founder Jenn Hampton's favorite pieces at these spots:

Sunset Pavilion Rubin45's *7800° Fahrenheit* includes three panels with geometric designs.

Carousel The circular floor mural by local artist Porkchop reads 'Good Thoughts, Good Words, Good Deeds' in five languages.

Steam Plant Ann Lewis' *Never Turn Your Back on the Ocean* is a 50ft mural in the windows of an inactive power plant.

Recommended by Jenn Hampton, *curator, Wooden Walls Project and Parlor Gallery,* @woodenwallsproject

37 Fire
ISLAND

LGBTIQ+ | SEASHORE | NIGHTLIFE

▬▬▬ Harried New Yorkers heave a collective sigh while boarding the ferry to Fire Island Pines – an LGBTIQ+ summer enclave hidden on a secluded sandbar 3 miles from Long Island's coastline. Cast off your city drag as soon as the boat docks to join Speedo-clad sun-worshippers participating in the daily bacchanal at this seasonal Brigadoon.

ATLANTIDE PHOTOTRAVEL/GETTY IMAGES ©

🖾 How To

Getting here Take the LIRR train line from Penn Station to Sayville and catch the shuttle bus to Sayville Ferry Terminal. The ferry is the only way on and off the island. Purchase round-trip tickets from machines or attendants for $40.25.

As an alternative, drive or take the Bay Bus to the ferry station. Budget 2½ hours.

When to go Between Memorial Day and Labor Day.

Top tip Bring any essentials you want for your stay. Resources like food are limited and expensive.

GLYN GENIN/ALAMY STOCK PHOTO ©

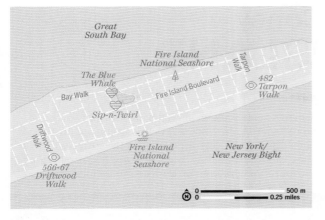

Great
South Bay

Fire Island
National Seashore

Tarpon
Walk

The Blue
Whale

Bay Walk

Fire Island Boulevard

482
Tarpon
Walk

Sip-n-Twirl

Driftwood
Walk

Fire Island
National
Seashore

New York/
New Jersey Bight

566-67
Driftwood
Walk

500 m
0.25 miles

Beach bums Start your day at the **Fire Island National Seashore** – a pristine beach linking meandering dunes and maritime forests. After a couple of hours spent soaking up vitamin D, some visitors trek west toward the Meat Rack – a scrubby woodland where gay men hunt for lascivious activities.

Dream homes Wander the boardwalks to drool over the muscular exteriors of modernist buildings built in the '60s and '70s by architects like Horace Gifford, who designed 63 of the area's roughly 600 homes. Peep at the entrances to **566–67 Driftwood Walk** or **482 Tarpon Walk** to admire how Gifford used cedar and glass to complement the natural surroundings.

Happy hour As night descends, Pavlovian conditioning overtakes the Pines. Five o'clock means Low Tea, a tradition dating back to 1966, where gaggles of boys babble over cocktails at the **Blue Whale**. At 8pm follow the crowd as it flows to the adjacent pool deck for High Tea – a distinctly more saturnalian affair. Finally, at 10pm, everyone disperses to eat dinner, take disco naps, or catch the last ferry to the mainland. All boardwalks eventually lead back to **Sip-n-Twirl** for an all-night dance fête.

Top left Houses, Fire Island National Seashore **Bottom left** Flags, Fire Island ferry dock

🏃 Island Culture

You are coming into a community that has been established for many years. Fire Island is a gay utopia that allows us to be who we are, completely. There's sexual freedom; there's queer freedom. It's about letting go of our jaded New York facade. Embrace and enjoy what the island has to offer.

By Pixie Aventura, *NYC-based drag queen who performs a solo show at the Pines Pavilion throughout summer and in Manhattan year-round, @pixieaventura*

38

Coney
ISLAND

ECCENTRIC | NOSTALGIC | OUTDOORS

▬▬▬ Walk down Coney Island's boardwalk on a sweltering day, and you'll see a mix of kitschy icons. Tattooed mermaids, vintage roller coasters and greasy food stands have greeted a colorful sea of New Yorkers since the 19th century. But visit during one of Coney Island's annual festivals, and you'll see something unique — the faded glamour of Brooklyn's 'riviera' returned to its former glory.

HOLLY VEGTER/SHUTTERSTOCK ©

🗺 How To

Getting here Take the D, F, N or Q to Coney Island-Stillwell Ave. One hour from Midtown Manhattan.

When to go The biggest festivals happen in June, July and January. Visit between Memorial Day and Labor Day to enjoy

the roller coasters. The boardwalk is open year-round.

Ride passes Coney Island has two main amusement parks, and they require separate entrance fees: Deno's Wonder Wheel Park and Luna Park, which has most of the rides.

AUTOMATIX6/SHUTTERSTOCK ©

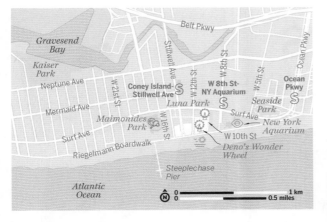

Top left Coney Island boardwalk
Bottom left Mermaid Parade

Find Your Festival

Mermaid Parade Sirens of the sea trade their fins for feet at the Mermaid Parade, an annual summer solstice celebration started in 1983. Ariel fans beware: this gritty festival isn't a Disney sing-along – it's an offbeat explosion of artistic expression that skews more Mardi Gras than Mickey Mouse. Blend in with the crowds along Surf Ave to see homemade floats, or don your craziest nautical fashions to compete in the best-dressed competition. Glitter, body paint and an open mind are all that's required to win.

Hot-dog-eating contest Join thousands of strong-stomached spectators on the corner of Stillwell and Surf every Fourth of July to watch **Nathan's Famous Hot Dog Eating Contest**. The annual spectacle pits wiener-eating wizards against one another in a battle to see who downs the most dogs in 10 minutes. The first recorded event occurred in 1972, but legend says the tradition dates to 1916, when Nathan Handwerker established the business.

Polar bear plunge Wash away last year's woes by plunging into the icy Atlantic with the **Coney Island Polar Bear Club**, founded in 1903. Every January 1st, thousands of New Yorkers join the warm-blooded crew near Coney Island's boardwalk for a refreshing start to the new year.

☺ The Mayor's Tips

For mermaids Hip Brooklyn parents use the Mermaid Parade for sex education, but consider staying home if you're a little bit prudish.

For wieners If you get inspired to run your own hot-dog-eating contest, dunk the bun in a cup of water and swish the hot dog casing in your hand. It'll save you lots of time and effort.

For polar bears That part of the body men are afraid will shrink isn't the problem. The real problem is that your toes will be numb for hours afterward. Wear into the ocean a pair of shoes you don't mind ruining.

By Dick Zigun, unofficial 'Mayor' of Coney Island, and founder and artistic director of Coney Island USA, @dickzigun

SIGHTS
of Coney Island

01 Walk the waterfront

Riegelmann Boardwalk, a 2.5-mile wood-plank walkway dating back to 1923, serves as the main thoroughfare between the beach and the rides.

02 Find the funny face

The toothy grin of Tillie, once the logo for the now-demolished Steeplechase Park, is an everlasting symbol of Coney Island quirk.

03 Brave the Cyclone

This rickety wooden roller coaster took its first 85ft plunge in 1927.

04 Nathan's Famous Franks

In 1916 Polish immigrant Nathan Handwerker started hawking his now-famous hot dogs for a nickel on the corner of Surf and Stillwell.

05 Thrash on the Thunderbolt

This 2234ft-long coaster writhes like a sea monster as it whirls passengers at 56mph.

06 Deep-sea diving

Wander through the New York Aquarium's coral reef tunnel to see black-tip reef sharks and over 100 other species.

07 Coney's oldest attraction

Views of the Jersey Shore and Manhattan appear while spinning

around the Wonder Wheel, built in 1920.

08 Try local brews

Take a tour of Coney Island Brewing Company's craft-beer facility before sipping on a summery Mermaid Pilsner.

09 Brooklyn's Eiffel Tower

Stand underneath the defunct Parachute Jump, a 250ft-tall landmark designed for the 1939 New York World's Fair and relocated here in 1941.

10 Beach baseball

Enjoy ocean views while watching the minor-league Brooklyn Cyclones play ball at Maimonides Park.

11 See a sideshow

A sword-swallower and a fire-eater are just a couple of the weird and wonderful acts in the Coney Island Circus Sideshow.

12 Gone fishing

Rough-and-tumble fishermen from all walks of life set up their poles along Steeplechase Pier to wait for the next big catch.

13 Coney Island Beach

Find a spot along Coney Island's 3 miles of sugar-sand beaches and watch cotton-candy clouds float overhead.

39

Storm King Art
CENTER

ART | NATURE | MOUNTAINS

Hike around the Hudson Valley's rolling hills at this pastoral art park located 60 miles north of New York City. Huge sculptures sprout from Storm King's 500 acres of groomed woodlands and meadows, blurring the line between human handiwork and nature. Scope out the scenery in autumn, when the surrounding forests put on an arboreal art show worthy of their own exhibition.

CORY SEAMER/SHUTTERSTOCK ©

How To

Getting here Driving is best if you want to explore areas surrounding the center. By train, take the Metro-North Hudson Line from Grand Central to Beacon, where Storm King provides round-trip shuttle services on weekends. Coach USA offers a direct bus service from Port Authority.

When to go Open early April to mid-December. Each season provides a unique canvas for the collection.

Top tips Pack a picnic, dress for the weather and plan on walking for a few hours.

BEAU BERRY/SHUTTERSTOCK ©

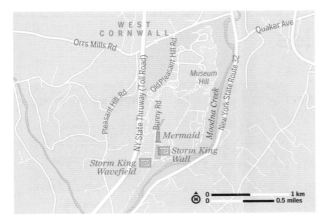

West Cornwall, Orrs Mills Rd, Quaker Ave, Old Pleasant Hill Rd, Pleasant Hill Rd, NY State Thruway (Toll Road), Bunny Rd, Moodna Creek, New York State Route 32, Museum Hill, Mermaid, Storm King Wall, Storm King Wavefield

0   1 km
0   0.5 miles

Top left and bottom left Storm King Art Center

DAY TRIPS EXPERIENCES

Panoramic peak Climb to the top of **Museum Hill**, the center's highest plateau, to enjoy expansive views and see the bulk of the center's offerings. A restored French Normandy-style chateau, built in 1935, serves as a gallery space and museum shop. Ionic columns from a 19th-century mansion frame nearby Schunnemunk Mountain.

Art and nature Seek out sublime sculptures that intentionally interact with the landscape. Get swept away in Maya Lin's *Storm King Wavefield*, an 11-acre earthwork of hills that undulate like the Hudson Highlands. Lose yourself in the passing clouds reflected in Sarah Sze's *Fallen Sky*, a ground-bound, 36ft-wide sphere made of stainless steel. Follow Andy Goldsworthy's 2278ft-long *Storm King Wall* as it snakes through trees, slips into a pond and makes a mad dash for the property's edge.

Local flora and fauna Stay vigilant while ambling along native grasslands, creeks and allées to spot deer, box turtles and cottontail rabbits. Canadian geese have an affinity for the weeping willows surrounding Roy Lichtenstein's *Mermaid*, and 80 other bird species can be seen soaring throughout the park.

Fall foliage Summer's verdant forests become a riot of reds, yellows and oranges between mid-September and mid-October, the prime time for regional leaf-peeping. Consult the annual Fall Foliage Prediction Map (smokymountain.com) to plan a peak-season trip.

Nearby Towns & Trails

Storm King is a stone's throw from stylish hamlets and rewarding hikes. Tack on one of these stops for a full-day affair with the Hudson Valley.

Beacon Hang in this hip haven for ex-Brooklynites and tour the Dia Beacon, a Nabisco factory turned contemporary-art complex.

Cold Spring Peruse the boutiques along Main St in this quaint spot with Americana appeal.

Breakneck Ridge Ramble through thick forests to rocky outcroppings on this strenuous hike overlooking the Hudson River.

Storm King Mountain Circle the crown of the art center's namesake mountain for a bird's-eye view of the region.

Practicalities

ARRIVING

208

GETTING AROUND

210

ACCOMMODATIONS

212

SAFE TRAVEL

214

MONEY

215

RESPONSIBLE TRAVEL

216

ESSENTIALS

218

EASY STEPS FROM THE AIRPORT TO THE CITY CENTER

When booking your tickets, John F Kennedy (JFK) and LaGuardia (LGA) airports, both in Queens, are the two main entry points for flights into NYC for international and regional flights. Both airports have similar amenities, but JFK has a bigger selection of restaurants. Some travelers arrive via the nearby Newark (EWR) airport in New Jersey and can travel to Manhattan via NJ Transit.

AT THE AIRPORT

PIT STOCK/SHUTTERSTOCK ©

Currency exchange booths are located at various terminals before exiting the airport to save time. Another option is to take out money from one of the ATMs at the airport to get U.S cash with an acceptable debit or credit card.

Travelers can take the **AirTrain** at JFK to connect to public transport hubs for $7.75. This price does not include the fare to board onward public transportation.

Charging stations are located throughout the concourses and retail lounge seating areas. In EWR, charging stations are usually only located by the gates.

Wi-fi is complimentary throughout the airports.

Travelex ATMs can be found at all terminals upon exit.

Customs and immigration Allow up to three hours to clear US customs and immigration upon arrival at either airport; this can change due to traffic and seasonal calendar. The US Visa Waiver Program covers visitors from many countries – including EU nations, the UK, Australia and New Zealand – but they will need to complete an online pre-authorization called an ESTA (esta.cbp.dhs.gov).

GETTING TO THE CITY CENTER

JFK Take the AirTrain to Jamaica station. From there, take the LIRR to 34th St-Penn station; it's a 15- to 20-minute ride. You can also take the E train from Jamaica into Manhattan for $2.75, but it's much longer. Another option is taking the Air-Train to Howard Beach station to transfer to the A train.

LaGuardia Take the M60 bus to 125th St and Lexington Ave in Harlem, then transfer to the 4/5/6 trains for other city destinations. You can also take the Q70 bus to Woodside station, then transfer to the LIRR to 34th St-Penn Station.

HOW MUCH FOR A...

taxi from JFK to Manhattan
$52

AirTrain Ticket
$7.75

LIRR Ticket to Penn Station
$7.75

Taxis from JFK and LaGuardia
From JFK yellow cabs have a $52 flat rate fee to Manhattan; from LaGuardia they average $24 to $44.

Taxi stands There are taxi pick-up stands for those who don't want a ride via an app service.

Ridesharing tips Every airport has specific pick-up spots for travelers to meet rideshares through Uber and Lyft. These spots can be an extra walk when exiting the airport. Locate where pick-ups are first before calling for a driver, as there is only a limited amount of time that the driver can wait for you.

NEW YORK CITY ARRIVING

OTHER POINTS OF ENTRY

Newark Liberty International Airport (EWR) is located in New Jersey, but is still a viable point of entry to NYC.

Accessing NYC from Newark via taxi is costly ($90 to $125). Instead catch the AirTrain to Newark Liberty Airport NJ Transit station then take any train going to New York Penn Station. Expect to pay $15.25, as your ticket will include access to the AirTrain and NJ Transit. If your NYC accommodations are below 34th St, transfer at Newark Penn Station (the first stop after Newark Airport along the NJ Transit) to switch to the PATH station that takes you along different stops in Lower Manhattan. The fare is the same rate as MTA buses and trains.

If you drive in, keep in mind there's a toll of roughly $10 to enter NYC from New Jersey, and be prepared for heavy traffic, especially between 4pm and 7pm.

TRANSPORT TIPS TO HELP YOU GET AROUND

NYC is among the most walkable cities in the US, so expect to spend a lot of time on your feet during the visit. However, that doesn't mean you have to spend the whole time walking. The city has an intricate subway system that stretches across four boroughs.

IMPROMPTU SHOWS

Subway travel often means encountering street dancers and performers, especially in high-traffic spots like Times Square. Be vigilant when opening your wallet to tip them.

SUBWAY ELEVATORS

Many less busy stations don't have access to an elevator. Check elevator status on the MTA website (new.mta.info/elevator-escalator-status) prior to travel.

One-way subway trip $2.75

FREE

AirTrain ticket $7.75

Download Citymapper and MTA apps

CARLESS TRAVEL

Parking can be inconvenient and pricey, so don't rent a car unless you plan to visit far-flung neighborhoods with poor public transport options.

OUTSIDE MANHATTAN

Take advantage of public transport to visit destinations outside NYC, such as day trips to Long Island or upstate New York.

WEEKEND SUBWAY

Subway schedules change on weekends. Many trains re-route and even skip stations outside the city center on Saturdays and Sundays. Allow extra time.

STREET CLOSURES

Summer street closures are common to accommodate outdoor seating and street fairs. Be prepared to re-route if taking a taxi, rideshare or bus.

TIP Watch out for signage telling you which trains take you downtown or uptown. At some stations, it's confusing.

ESSENTIAL MAPS & APPS

Download the Citymapper and MTA apps for directions on how to get to any establishment using trains or subway. The MTA app is better for bus routes and gives you accurate times for the next bus. The Curbed app lets you request yellow taxis if you don't want to use Uber or Lyft.

SUBWAY ESSENTIALS

Ticketing machines Use cash or credit card to get a Metrocard to use for your stay. Most single-ride bus and subway fares are $2.75. At subway stations there will be a turnstile to enter the platforms where you can swipe for entry. In most stations,

there'll be an attendant in a booth who you can go to for assistance or who can add more cash onto your Metrocard if the machine isn't working. You won't be able to enter without a swipe. For longer stays, consider purchasing a weekly or monthly card for unlimited rides.

1/2/3 & 4/5/6 trains These subway lines will take you to most Manhattan tourist destinations, and their schedules tend to be the most reliable for service within the borough. Letter lines like the A, B, C, or E lines tend to have the most weekend interruptions.

Begging It's not uncommon to see people going through the subway cars asking for money and sitting on the platforms. To avoid giving offence, don't stare. If you're asked for money, it's fine to politely decline and keep moving.

Busy hubs Hubs such as 34th St-Penn station, World Trade Center or 42nd St-Times Sq will often have a pronounced police presence and lots of tourist traffic.

Crowded carriages Trains can get crowded, especially during rush hour. Be considerate of people's space. If you're standing, hold your bag in front of you and if you are sitting, do not take up the next seat with your belongings. It's customary to give up your seat to the elderly, though this practice is not enforced as strictly on trains as it is on the bus.

UNIQUE AND LOCAL WAYS TO STAY

New York has no shortage of hotels, ranging from opulent five-stars to budget-friendly hostels. Neighborhoods like Chelsea, Midtown and SoHo are home to more expensive hotels. You can find smaller, budget-conscious hotels in neighborhoods like Murray Hill or Hell's Kitchen, but there are also some scattered around other areas.

Find a place to stay in New York City

HOW MUCH FOR A NIGHT IN A...

budget hotel
from $108

midrange hotel
from $299

centrally located Airbnb rental
from $150

LUXURY HOTELS

Luxury hotels are plentiful throughout Manhattan, and each – such as Baccarat in Midtown or the Carlyle Hotel on the Upper East Side – comes with an array of first-class amenities.

MIDRANGE HOTELS

The Times Square EDITION offers stunning city views, and the Standard Hotel in the Meatpacking District is also a popular nightlife spot. Arlo SoHo and the Dominick are in the posh downtown area and have great rooftop lounges and restaurants.

BUDGET HOTELS

Chains like Holiday Inn or Hampton Suites are widespread; check their websites for a list of locations. The Jane is a stylish West Village option, with a great location by public transport and nightlife.

AIRBNB & APARTMENT RENTALS

While there are plenty of apartment listings in NYC, short-term rentals are illegal in multifamily buildings, so you won't be able to stay longer than 30 days. Prices are comparable to budget or midrange hotels.

BOOKING

Spring and summer are the hardest and most expensive times to book a hotel room, so try to book by early April before the price increases. Holiday season between November and December is also busy, so book before early September. Consider booking directly with hotels, as this may result in better service and rates than booking via third-party sites. Useful website:

NYC (nycgo.com/hotels) Loads of listings from the NYC Official Guide.

HOSTELS

There are a few hostels in Manhattan with prime locations, such as Jazz on the Park Hostel near Central Park or the HI New York City Hostel near Lincoln Center.

WHERE TO STAY, IF YOU LOVE...

→ **Museums, culture and history** Upper West Side (p30) Steps away from Central Park and home to the Museum of Natural History.

Shopping, theater and entertainment Midtown (p46) The home of Madison Square Garden and Broadway, among other things.

Film, arts and culture Chelsea & Greenwich Village (p64) Home to the city's largest LGBTIQ+ community and the city's premier art-gallery destination. What's not to love?

Legacy, restaurants and entertainment Tribeca & the Financial District (p86) Tribeca and the FiDi combine historical sites with a plethora of trendy bars and restaurants.

Fashion, food and history SoHo & Chinatown (p98) SoHo is synonymous with fashion and shopping; Chinatown with great food and the imprint of the Chinese-American community.

↓ **Murals, trendsetters and restaurants** Brooklyn (p114) The one borough that rivals Manhattan for its selection of restaurants. Also a haven for creatives with its colorful street murals and trendy neighborhoods.

Vintage, arts and hipsterism East Village & the Lower East Side (p132) Whether you're up for a vintage rock venue, open-mike poetry slam, quirky museum or an offbeat restaurant, these neighborhoods have you covered.

Wealth, shopping and museums Upper East Side (p150) Home of old-money residents in historic buildings across from Central Park, this neighborhood will make you feel like you're one of the elite.

History, entertainment and culture Harlem (p166) This prolific African American neighborhood will show you a good time with the Apollo Theater and plenty of bars and jazz clubs.

Diversity, museums and arts Queens (p180) As one of NYC's most diverse areas, you can feel like you've traveled through several countries in just a couple of train stops.

Far left Times Square EDITION **Above** American Museum of Natural History **Near left** Smorgasburg, Williamsburg, Brooklyn

SAFE TRAVEL

Like any city, it's best to be alert whenever traveling in NYC, especially when navigating subway stations and dense pedestrian traffic. In the winter, wear proper cold-weather boots to avoid slipping on ice.

HEALTH If you need to seek medical attention during your trip, you can visit an urgent care center where no insurance is required and will cost an out-of-pocket fee for a doctor to come visit your hotel room or rental.

WALLET SAFETY Be vigilant when opening your wallet or purse when tipping street performers.

TAXIS & RIDESHARES Always double-check to make sure you are entering the right vehicle.

COVID-19
At time of writing, restrictions were enforced throughout the city and proof of vaccination was required to enter restaurants and other establishments. For up-to-date info, search for 'coronavirus' on nycgo.com.

PHARMACIES
Pharmacies are easily accessible and offer over-the-counter medications. They will also stock store-brand medications at a lower price than name brands.

MARIAKRAY/SHUTTERSTOCK ©

SAMFOTOGRAFY/SHUTTERSTOCK ©

Police officers are a common sight in the subway and around tourist areas such as Times Square. You may even see them on horseback in certain areas in Midtown.

LOST ON THE SUBWAY
Go to the middle car of the train to find the conductor, who usually pokes his head out the window, or go to an attendant near the subway turnstile.

QUICK TIPS TO HELP YOU MANAGE YOUR MONEY

CURRENCY
US dollar

HOW MUCH FOR A...

glass of wine
$10

lunch for two
$35 to $40

week's Metrocard
$33

MONEY SAVERS
For longer stays, buy an unlimited weekly Metrocard ($33) rather than pay per ride. Take advantage of the common 4pm to 7pm happy hour at many establishments. For museums and cultural institutions, check the website to see what days they offer free admission.

CREDIT CARDS
Major credit cards are widely accepted almost everywhere. Some smaller businesses, street fairs or outdoor markets may prefer cash, so carry some with you.

ATMS
ATMs are common and can be found in any deli or local pharmacy. Each has different fees for withdrawals.

PAYING THE BILL
Dine-in eateries generally bring you a receipt at the end of the meal. Bars will ask if you want to open a tab if you plan on having multiple drinks or are with friends.

MONEY CHANGERS
Always try to change your currency into US dollars at the airports for the best rate. Keep in mind that it's cheaper to take cash out of an ATM than to change money at a foreign exchange office, especially at tourist hubs such as Times Square. You can also exchange money at any local bank for an additional charge.

TIPPING
Tipping is not optional; only withhold tips in cases of outrageously bad service.
Restaurant servers 18–20%
Bartenders Minimum per drink $1, per specialty cocktail $2, or 15–20% overall
Taxi drivers 10–15%
Airport and hotel porters $2 per bag, minimum per cart $5
Hotel cleaners $2–4 per night

DISCOUNT CARDS
Several discount cards save tourists money when visiting major attractions (nycgo.com/things-to-do/tours-in-nyc/attraction-passes). Save up to 45% off tickets with the Explorer Pass. A CityPASS also offers major discounts at various shops and attractions.

RESPONSIBLE TRAVEL

Positive, sustainable and feel-good experiences around the city.

CHOOSE SUSTAINABLE VENUES

For cocktails with a secret garden aesthetic, the Met Rooftop garden offers a different ambience where patrons can enjoy art alongside nice views of the city.

The New York Botanical Garden is worth the trip to see the brilliant exhibits and displays dedicated to a variety of plant species and flowers. The Brooklyn Botanical Garden is another sight worth visiting for nature-lovers.

Take a tour at the Jacob Javits Center's Green Roof, which is home to 17 species of birds and 300,000 honeybees. The green roof also reduces the center's energy consumption.

Walk along the High Line, in the Meatpacking District, for a unique perspective on public landscapes.

GIVE BACK

Give out groceries and meals to low-income families with City Harvest (cityharvest.org) and Citymeals-On-Wheels (citymeals.org).

Learn about NYC's various bird species and how to protect them with Audubon New York (ny.audubon.org).

Make backpacks with food and essentials for the homeless at Backpacks for the Street (backpacksforthestreet.org).

Protect the local environment by volunteering with NYC Parks to keep the city safe and clean for visitors and the community.

Above High Line. **Right** Citi Bikes.
OLIVER FOERSTNER/SHUTTERSTOCK ©

SUPPORT LOCAL

For fresh produce sourced from local farms, visit one of the city's many green-markets, such as the one in Union Square. These markets are spread throughout the boroughs and offer everything from fresh produce to homemade condiments such as honey or maple syrup. Market schedule and locations can be found online (grownyc.org).

Local Roots Market & Cafe is a small eatery in Brooklyn that specializes in menu items with ingredients from local farms.

LEARN MORE

Explore NYC's multitude of diverse neighborhoods, where it's common to see store signage in different languages and hear other languages spoken.

Attend a cultural festival such as West Indian Day Parade (September) or Puerto Rican Day Parade (June).

Visit the Schomburg Center of Black Research (p173) to learn about the African American figures who helped shape Harlem.

GET AROUND

Carry a reusable water bottle and a tote bag to grab small items instead of using a plastic bag. They are commonly sold at local shops and supermarkets throughout the city.

Rent a Citi Bike for environmentally friendly city travel. Bike stations are sprinkled throughout the different boroughs. Day passes cost $15, and a single ride costs $3.50 for 30 minutes.

S-F/SHUTTERSTOCK ©

CLIMATE CHANGE & TRAVEL

It's impossible to ignore the impact we have when traveling, and the importance of making changes where we can. Lonely Planet urges all travelers to engage with their travel carbon footprint. There are many carbon calculators online that allow travelers to estimate the carbon emissions generated by their journey; try resurgence.org/resources/carbon-calculator.html. Many airlines and booking sites offer travelers the option of offsetting the impact of greenhouse gas emissions by contributing to climate-friendly initiatives around the world. We continue to offset the carbon footprint of all Lonely Planet staff travel, while recognizing this is a mitigation more than a solution.

RESOURCES

citymapper.com
nycgo.com
new.mta.info
ferry.nyc

NEW YORK CITY POSITIVE-IMPACT TRAVEL

ESSENTIAL NUTS-AND-BOLTS

NO DRIVING
Don't bother renting a car unless you plan on day-tripping outside city limits. Instead purchase a Metrocard and download essential rideshare apps.

YELLOW CABS
It's common to hail yellow cabs on the street wherever you are in Manhattan, but you can also request one through the Curbed app.

SMOKING IN OUTDOOR AREAS
You cannot smoke in public parks or outdoor dining areas at restaurants or bars.

FAST FACTS

Time Zone
GMT-5

Country Code
+1

Electricity
120/240V
60Hz

GOOD TO KNOW

The drinking age is 21 for all establishments selling alcohol or spirits. Many will ask for ID upon entry.

Marijuana is legal within NYC; however, it's still illegal to sell recreational weed.

Tipping is expected and customary at dine-in restaurants. It's normal to tip between 18% and 20% of your bill.

For groups larger than four, some eateries automatically add their tip to the receipt.

A city tax gets applied to all purchases.

ACCESSIBLE TRAVEL

Wheelchair-accessible platforms aren't availabile at every subway station. Check the the MTA website (new.mta.info/accessibility/stations) for information.

Subway elevators do not always work. Check the MTA website (new.mta.info/elevator-escalator-status).

MTA buses are wheelchair accessible and often a better option than the subway.

Theatre Access NYC (theatreaccess.nyc) can help you find Broadway shows with special accommodations.

To request a wheelchair-accessible yellow cab, call (646) 599-9999 or text a request to (646) 400-0789. If you can't catch a taxi, contact NYC Wheelchair Transportation (nycwheelchairtransportation.com; 212-705-8773) for assistance.

The NYC government website (nyc.gov) has disability-specific resources.

ACCESSIBLE HOTELS

To check for hotels with wheelchair accessibility, you can search the Wheelchair Jimmy (wheelchairjimmy.com) database.

MUSEUM PROGRAMS

Check different museum schedules for special programs for visitors with autism.

ON THE SUBWAY

Passengers tend to give up their seats for children, but if no seats are available huddle together. Move away from doors when people are exiting and stay by a pole.

FAMILY TRAVEL

Base yourselves near a train station and plan your day around what's close to the subway to shorten walking time.

Stay in residential areas away from Midtown or tourist areas to avoid crowds. It's also quieter for kids to fall asleep without disruption.

Book tickets ahead of time and be aware of age requirements at establishments where alcohol is served.

Use the crosswalk when you're on foot and make sure to hold your child's hand, especially in crowds.

PUBLIC TOILETS

Most establishments won't let you use their bathrooms without paying for something first. You can find restrooms at major transit hubs like Penn Station or Grand Central Terminal and city parks.

FAMILY-FRIENDLY HOTELS

Stay at hotels that accommodate larger families like the TRYP by Wyndham in Times Square or the Residence Inn New York Manhattan, with their larger suites and amenities for traveling families like extra cribs or babysitting. Contact your hotel to see if they provide services for those traveling with infants or toddlers.

LGBTIQ+ TRAVELERS

East Village and West Village have notable LGBTIQ+ establishments. The West Village is the center of LGBTIQ+ culture and includes Stonewall Inn, which was at the center of the gay-rights movements.

Visit the Leslie-Lohman Museum of Gay and Lesbian Art, which showcases artwork that depicts the LGBTIQ+ experience.

Fire Island (p198) is a popular summer day trip for LGBTIQ+ travelers. Take the LIRR Montauk Branch to Mastic/Shirley for the William Floyd Estate or to Bay Shore, Sayville or Patchogue to access ferry terminals.

Index

000 Map pages

000 Map pages

Our Writers

HARMONY DIFO

Harmony is a writer and editor specializing in lifestyle and culture journalism. Following roles in arts and media, she launched her writing and editorial business out of New York City and Johannesburg.

💻 @harmonydifo.com

My favourite experience is walking the streets of New York City's East Village.

JOHN GARRY

John is a Brooklyn-based writer and teacher. After growing up in the bucolic Catskill Mountains, he hightailed it to New York City and never looked back – aside from when he goes hiking, which is often.

📷 @garryjohnfrancis

My favourite experience is biking along the Hudson River on a spring day, breezing through the city as it blooms back to life.

DANA GIVENS

Dana is a travel and lifestyle journalist born and raised in New York City. When she isn't traveling the world, she enjoys reading a good book and visiting her favorite art galleries that she grew up with.

📷 @danawritesalot

My favourite experience is seeing the Upper East Side's hidden art gems away from the Met or the Guggenheim.

DEEPA LAKSHMIN

Deepa is a freelance writer who started out interning at magazines in Manhattan and has lived there ever since. As a journalist, she's reported for National Geographic, MTV News, and NYLON.

📷 @deepathedisco 🐦 @deepa

My favourite experience is relaxing on the swings at Pier 26 and watching the evening sunset over the water.

THIS BOOK

Design development
Lauren Egan, Tina García, Fergal Condon

Content development
Anne Mason

Cartography development
Wayne Murphy, Katerina Pavkova

Production development
Mario D'Arco, Dan Moore, Sandie Kestell, Virginia Moreno, Juan Winata

Series development leadership
Liz Heynes, Darren O'Connell, Piers Pickard, Chris Zeiher

Commissioning Editor
Daniel Bolger

Coordinating Editor
Simon Williamson

Product Editor
James Appleton

Cartographer
Rachel Imeson

Book Designer
Fergal Condon

Assisting Editors
Janet Austin, Gabrielle Stefanos

Cover Researcher
Lauren Egan

Thanks Gwen Cotter, Clare Healy, Karen Henderson, Sandie Kestell, Alison Killilea, Darren O'Connell, Sheeka Sanahori, John Taufa